First published in Great Britain 1989 by
The Parent and Child Programme
Michelin House, 81 Fulham Road,
London SW3 6RB

Published in association with LDA

© Octopus Publishing Group Ltd. 1989

ISBN 1-85270-119-6

Produced by Mandarin Offset
Printed and bound in Hong Kong

# First Dictionary

Educational adviser and compiler
## Dee Reid

Definitions by
## Deborah Manley

## This book belongs to

Heenal malde

Spelling Dictionary and cover illustrated by
## Tony Ross

Definition Dictionary illustrated by
## Gill Tomblin, Simon Burr, Robert Cooke, Norma Bergin, Martin Kingston

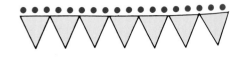

# To Parents

## About this dictionary

The *Parent and Child First Dictionary* is the result of the latest research by a leading educational team into the writing of children aged 7-9. The research was conducted by Learning Development Aids (LDA) in 1988 in association with the Reading Centre, at the University of Reading. Many samples from a wide selection of children's writing were examined and from these a comprehensive list of the words most frequently used by children in this age group was compiled. The top 3000+ of these words form the word list in this dictionary.

The *Parent and Child First Dictionary* is really two dictionaries in one. The first part is a *Spelling Dictionary* (page 3), to help your child to look up the spelling of a word quickly and easily. At this age, it is usually the *spelling* of a word *rather than the meaning* that a child needs to check. The second part of the dictionary is a *Definition Dictionary* (page 43). This will help your child to use words correctly.

A child who wants to know how to *spell* a word looks in the first part (the *Spelling Dictionary*, page 3); and a child who wants to know how to *use* a word looks first in the *Spelling Dictionary* and, if the word is printed in blue there, he or she knows the word also appears in the second part (the *Definition Dictionary*, page 43) in a sentence which makes clear its meaning.

## Helping your child

To use a dictionary your child needs to become familiar with three things in particular: **alphabetical order**, **handling a dictionary**, and **spelling**. As a parent you can do a lot to help your child master these skills.

▷ **alphabetical order**: playing word games will familiarize your child with alphabetical order. For example, try taking it in turns to name an animal a-z or playing "Granny went to Market" naming the items in alphabetical order (e.g. she bought an apple, some bread etc).

▷ **handling a dictionary**: explain that using a dictionary is different to reading a story-book (you don't have to read it from beginning to end; you can skip over pages). Try setting puzzles for each other (e.g. find the word "impossible" in 25 seconds!). This will help your child get used to flicking through the dictionary to find the correct starting letter and skim reading the entries to find the correct word.

▷ **spelling**: playing memory games with your child is a good way to practise since it builds up the necessary skills to retain letter patterns. For instance, suggest your child studies a word, turns the dictionary over and tries to write the word from memory. Your child can then turn the dictionary back again to check the results.

If your child cannot spell a word, rather than spelling the word letter by letter, encourage your child to take a closer look at the word itself: look at word patterns (e.g. "pass", "passage", "passenger"); break up words into sections (e.g. "con-fi-dent"); see words within words (e.g. "there" has the words "the", "he", "her", "here" inside it.

It is important to encourage your child to see the dictionary as a *positive* help and a tool for writing, rather than as something negative, or as an admission of some kind of failure in spelling ability. Your encouragement and interest will build your child's confidence about using a dictionary.

# The Spelling Dictionary

When children need help to write a word, more often than not, they already know its *meaning;* what they are not sure about is its *spelling.* This part of the dictionary is designed to help your child look up words he or she is unsure how to *spell* and to do this as quickly and easily as possible.

▷ over 3000 of the most frequently used words are listed

▷ words are listed in alphabetical order

▷ words are listed without definitions for quick and easy reference

▷ words printed in blue also appear in the *Definition Dictionary* because they may be confusing and a child would benefit from seeing the word used accurately in a sentence (pages 43-97).

All children's dictionaries can provide only a selection of vocabulary. The basis of the selection for this dictionary are those words which research has shown to be those most widely used by children aged 7-9. In making the selection we have tried to include the most usual form of words (for instance, we have both "waiter" and "waitress", but we have included only "postman" and not "postwoman").

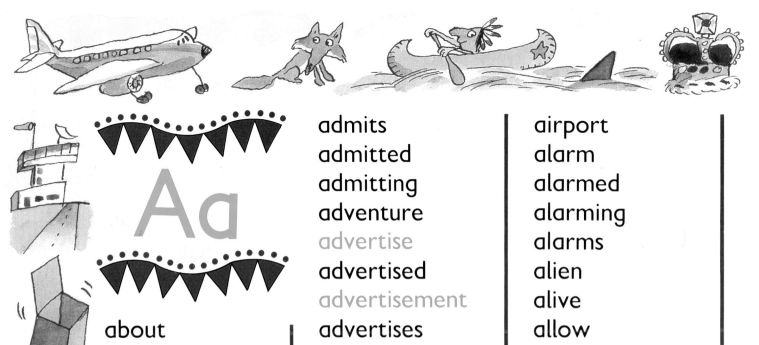

# Aa

about
accept
accepted
accepting
accepts
accident
achieve
achieved
achieves
achieving
acre
acrobat
across
address
addresses
admiration
admire
admired
admires
admiring
admit

admits
admitted
admitting
adventure
advertise
advertised
advertisement
advertises
advertising
advice
advise
advised
advises
advising
aerial
aeroplane
affect
afraid
after
afternoon
afterwards
again
against
agree
agreed
agreeing
agrees
air

airport
alarm
alarmed
alarming
alarms
alien
alive
allow
allowed
allowing
allows
almost
along
aloud
already
alright
altar
alter
although
altogether
always
amaze
amazed
amazement
amazes
amazing
ambulance
anger

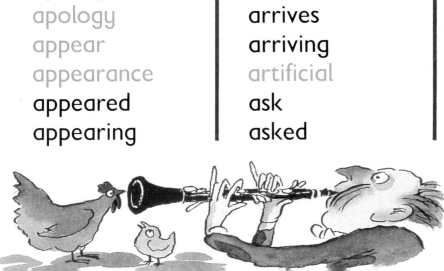

| | | |
|---|---|---|
| angrily | appears | asking |
| angry | apple | asks |
| animal | are | asleep |
| annoy | area | assemblies |
| annoyed | aren't | assembly |
| annoying | argue | assist |
| annoys | argued | assistance |
| another | argues | assisted |
| answer | arguing | assisting |
| answered | argument | assists |
| answering | arithmetic | astonish |
| answers | ark | astonished |
| anxiety | armies | astonishes |
| anxious | army | astonishing |
| anxiously | arrange | astonishment |
| anymore | arranged | astronaut |
| anyone | arrangement | ate |
| anything | arranges | attach |
| anyway | arranging | attached |
| apologize | around | attack |
| apologized | arrival | attacked |
| apologizes | arrive | attacking |
| apologizing | arrived | attacks |
| apology | arrives | attention |
| appear | arriving | audience |
| appearance | artificial | aunt |
| appeared | ask | aunty |
| appearing | asked | autumn |

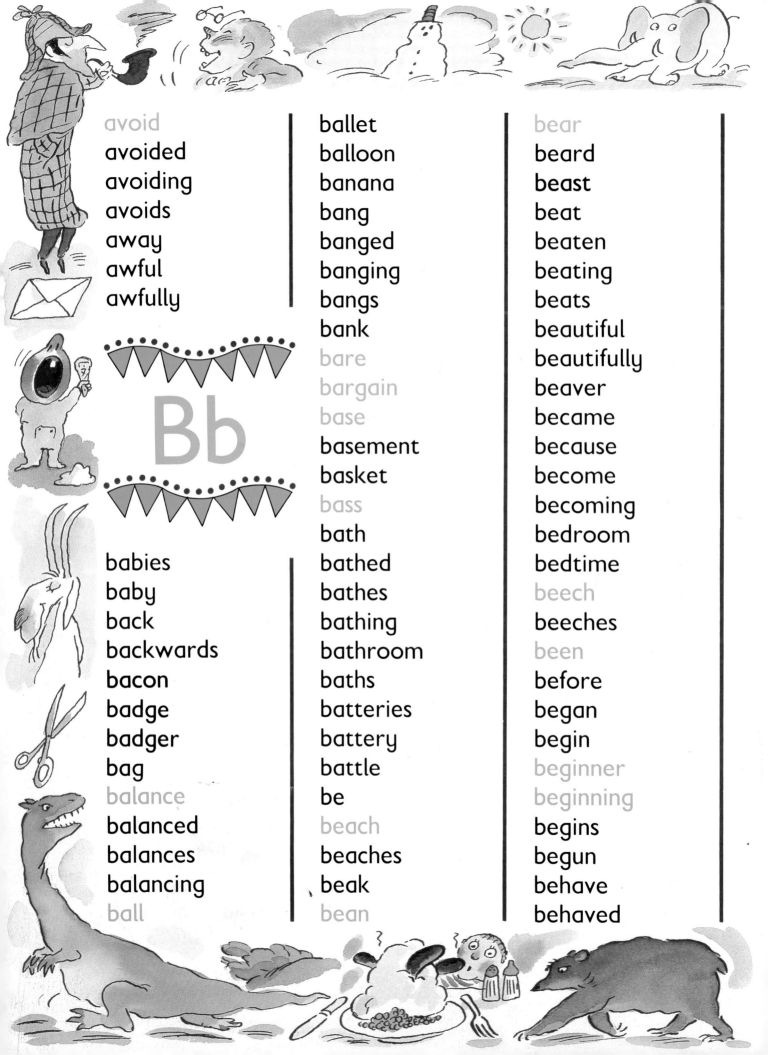

avoid
avoided
avoiding
avoids
away
awful
awfully

## Bb

babies
baby
back
backwards
bacon
badge
badger
bag
balance
balanced
balances
balancing
ball

ballet
balloon
banana
bang
banged
banging
bangs
bank
bare
bargain
base
basement
basket
bass
bath
bathed
bathes
bathing
bathroom
baths
batteries
battery
battle
be
beach
beaches
beak
bean

bear
beard
beast
beat
beaten
beating
beats
beautiful
beautifully
beaver
became
because
become
becoming
bedroom
bedtime
beech
beeches
been
before
began
begin
beginner
beginning
begins
begun
behave
behaved

| | | |
|---|---|---|
| behaves | bit | bold |
| behaving | bite | bolder |
| behaviour | bites | bomb |
| behind | biting | bone |
| being | bitten | bonfire |
| belief | black | book |
| believe | blew | boot |
| believed | blind | bore |
| believes | blizzard | bored |
| believing | blood | bores |
| bell | blow | boring |
| below | blowing | born |
| berry | blown | borne |
| berth | blows | both |
| beside | blue | bottle |
| best | board | bottom |
| better | boast | bough |
| between | boasted | bought |
| bicycle | boastful | boulder |
| big | boasting | bow |
| bigger | boasts | bowed |
| biggest | boat | bowing |
| bike | bodies | bowled |
| bikini | body | bows |
| bird | boil | box |
| birth | boiled | boxes |
| birthday | boiling | boy |
| biscuit | boils | braille |

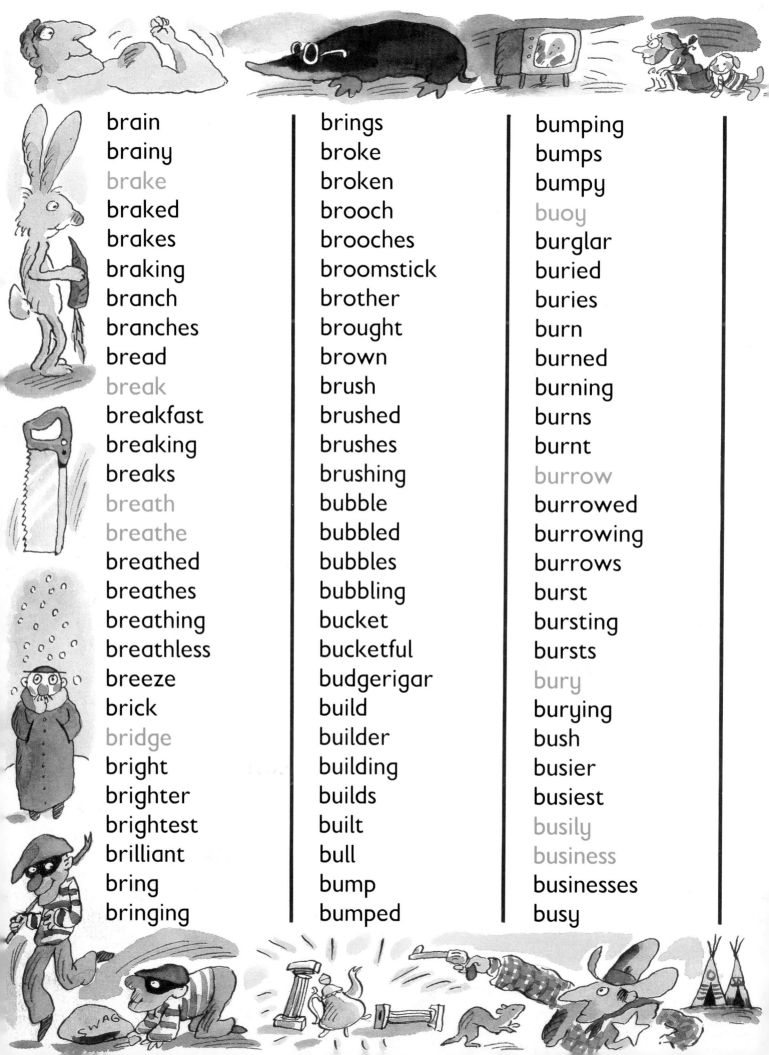

brain
brainy
brake
braked
brakes
braking
branch
branches
bread
break
breakfast
breaking
breaks
breath
breathe
breathed
breathes
breathing
breathless
breeze
brick
bridge
bright
brighter
brightest
brilliant
bring
bringing

brings
broke
broken
brooch
brooches
broomstick
brother
brought
brown
brush
brushed
brushes
brushing
bubble
bubbled
bubbles
bubbling
bucket
bucketful
budgerigar
build
builder
building
builds
built
bull
bump
bumped

bumping
bumps
bumpy
buoy
burglar
buried
buries
burn
burned
burning
burns
burnt
burrow
burrowed
burrowing
burrows
burst
bursting
bursts
bury
burying
bush
busier
busiest
busily
business
businesses
busy

butter
butterflies
butterfly
button
buy
buying
buys
buzz
buzzed
buzzes
buzzing
by
byte

# Cc

café
cage
cake
calculator
calendar
call
called

calling
calls
calm
came
camp
camped
camper
camping
camps
can
can't
canal
candle
canoe
cannot
capsize
capsized
capsizes
capsizing
captain
caravan
card
cardboard
care
cared
careful
carefully
careless

carelessly
cares
caring
carpet
carriage
carried
carries
carrot
carry
carrying
carve
carved
carves
carving
case
cassette
castle
catch
catches
catching
caterpillar
caught
cause
caused
causes
causing
cave
ceiling

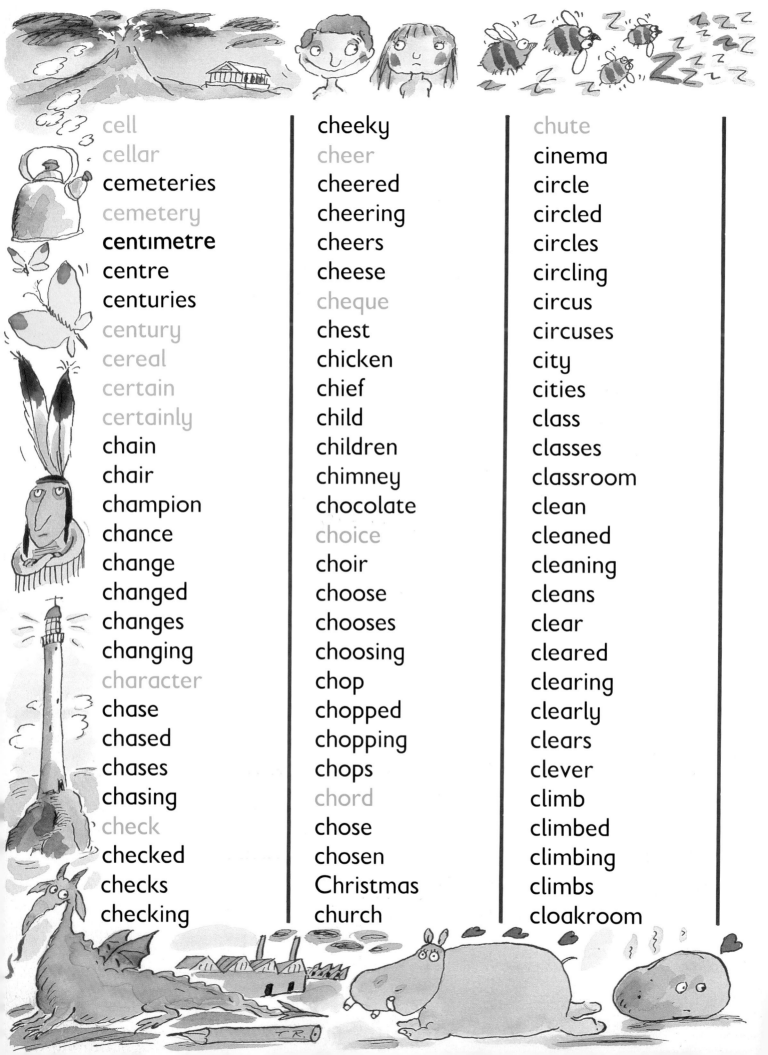

cell
cellar
cemeteries
cemetery
**centimetre**
centre
centuries
century
cereal
certain
certainly
chain
chair
champion
chance
change
changed
changes
changing
character
chase
chased
chases
chasing
check
checked
checks
checking

cheeky
cheer
cheered
cheering
cheers
cheese
cheque
chest
chicken
chief
child
children
chimney
chocolate
choice
choir
choose
chooses
choosing
chop
chopped
chopping
chops
chord
chose
chosen
Christmas
church

chute
cinema
circle
circled
circles
circling
circus
circuses
city
cities
class
classes
classroom
clean
cleaned
cleaning
cleans
clear
cleared
clearing
clearly
clears
clever
climb
climbed
climbing
climbs
cloakroom

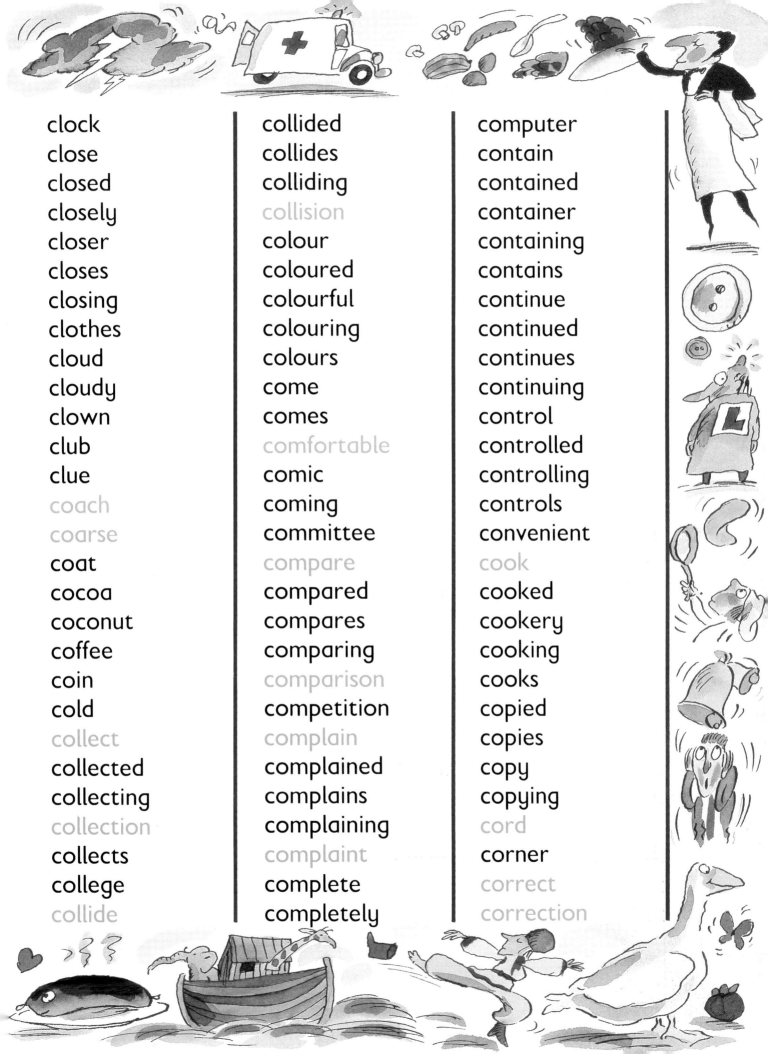

clock
close
closed
closely
closer
closes
closing
clothes
cloud
cloudy
clown
club
clue
coach
coarse
coat
cocoa
coconut
coffee
coin
cold
collect
collected
collecting
collection
collects
college
collide

collided
collides
colliding
collision
colour
coloured
colourful
colouring
colours
come
comes
comfortable
comic
coming
committee
compare
compared
compares
comparing
comparison
competition
complain
complained
complains
complaining
complaint
complete
completely

computer
contain
contained
container
containing
contains
continue
continued
continues
continuing
control
controlled
controlling
controls
convenient
cook
cooked
cookery
cooking
cooks
copied
copies
copy
copying
cord
corner
correct
correction

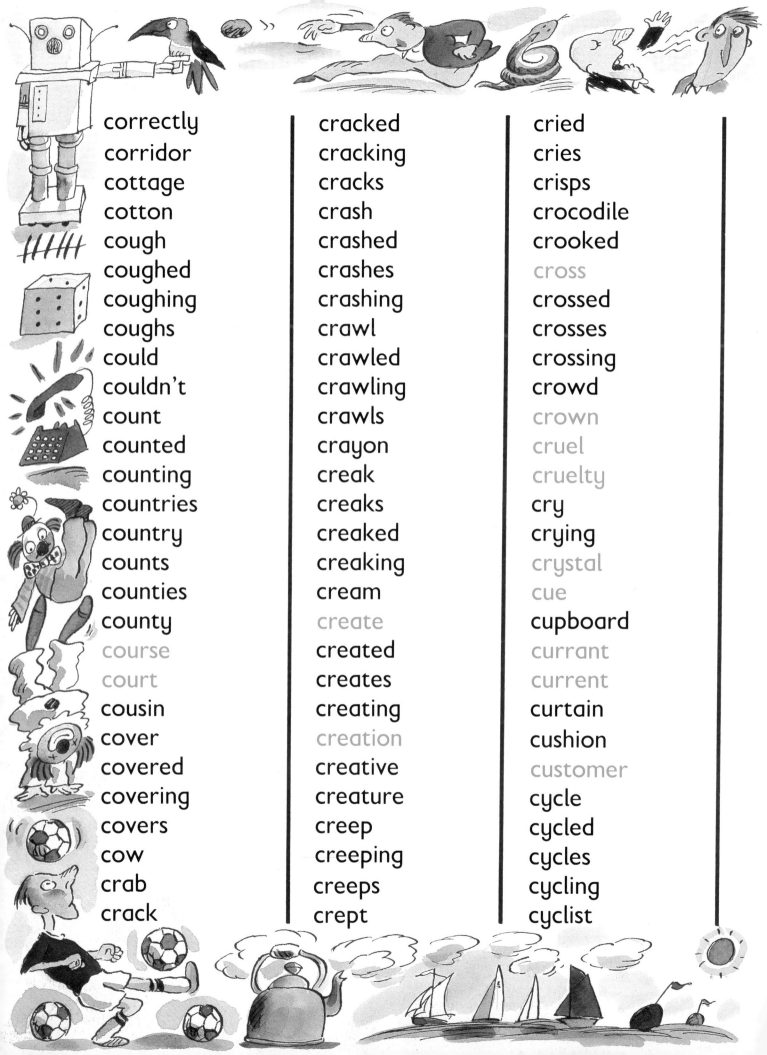

correctly
corridor
cottage
cotton
cough
coughed
coughing
coughs
could
couldn't
count
counted
counting
countries
country
counts
counties
county
course
court
cousin
cover
covered
covering
covers
cow
crab
crack

cracked
cracking
cracks
crash
crashed
crashes
crashing
crawl
crawled
crawling
crawls
crayon
creak
creaks
creaked
creaking
cream
create
created
creates
creating
creation
creative
creature
creep
creeping
creeps
crept

cried
cries
crisps
crocodile
crooked
cross
crossed
crosses
crossing
crowd
crown
cruel
cruelty
cry
crying
crystal
cue
cupboard
currant
current
curtain
cushion
customer
cycle
cycled
cycles
cycling
cyclist

# Dd

daddy
damage
damaged
damages
damaging
dance
danced
dancer
dances
dancing
danger
dangerous
dangerously
dare
dared
dares
daring
dark
darker
darkest
darkness

daughter
day
dead
deal
dealer
dealing
deals
dealt
dear
dearer
dearest
death
decide
decided
decides
deciding
decision
decorate
decorated
decorates
decorating
decoration
decorator
deep
deeper
deepest
deer
definite

definition
delay
delayed
delaying
delays
deliberate
deliberately
delicious
deliver
delivered
delivering
delivers
denied
denies
deny
denying
depend
depended
depending
depends
describe
described
describes
describing
description
desert
deserted
deserting

| | | |
|---|---|---|
| deserts | dirty | dives |
| design | disappear | divide |
| dessert | disappeared | divided |
| destroy | disappearing | divides |
| destroyed | disappears | dividing |
| destroying | disappoint | diving |
| destroys | disappointed | division |
| destruction | disappointing | doctor |
| detective | disappointment | doe |
| dew | disappoints | does |
| diamond | disco | doesn't |
| didn't | discover | doing |
| die | discovered | doll |
| died | discovering | dolly |
| dies | discovers | dolphin |
| difference | disguise | don't |
| different | disguised | donkey |
| difficult | disguises | door |
| difficulty | disguising | dormitory |
| dinner | disobedience | dormitories |
| dinosaur | disobey | double |
| direct | disobeyed | dough |
| directed | disobeying | down |
| directing | disobeys | downstairs |
| direction | distance | dragon |
| directs | dive | drank |
| dirtier | dived | draw |
| dirtiest | diver | drawer |

drawing
drawn
draws
dream
dreamed
dreaming
dreams
dress
dressed
dresses
dressing
drew
dried
dries
drink
drinking
drinks
drive
driver
drives
driving
drop
dropped
dropping
drops
drove
drunk
dry

drying
duck
due
dungeon
dust
dusted
dusting
dusts
dusty
dye
dyed
dyeing
dying

# Ee

each
eagle
ear
earlier
earliest
early
earn

earned
earning
earns
earth
easier
easiest
easily
Easter
easy
eat
eaten
eating
eats
edge
education
effect
eight
either
elephant
eleven
else
employer
emptied
empties
empty
emptying
end
ended

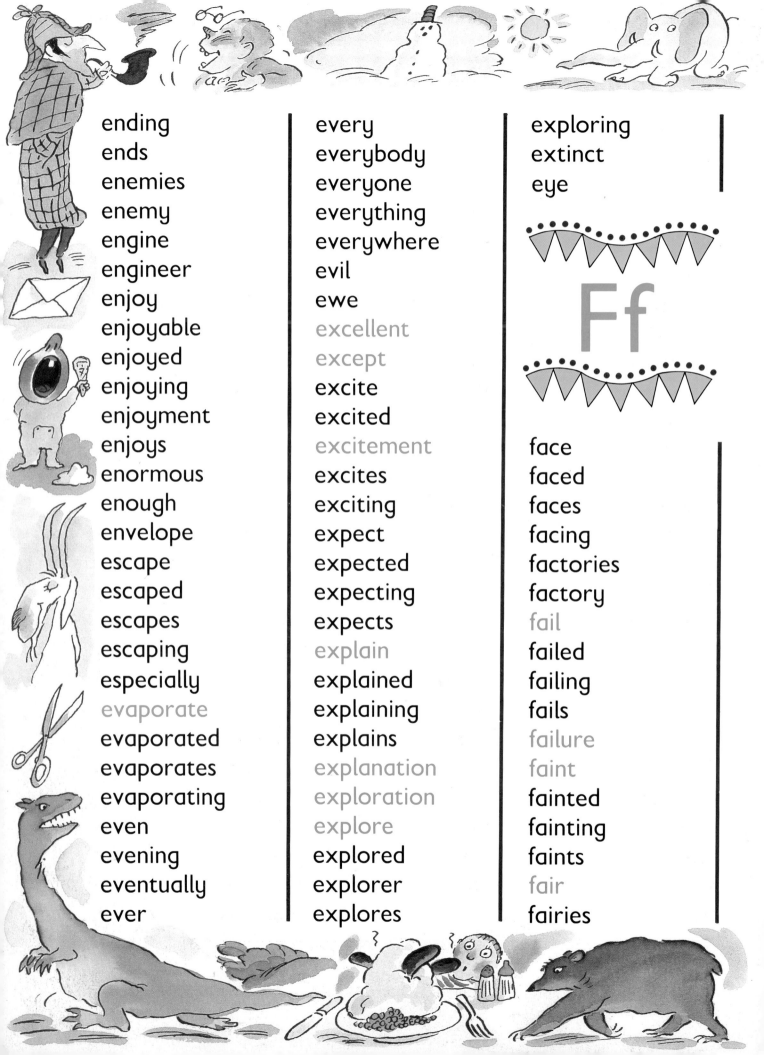

ending
ends
enemies
enemy
engine
engineer
enjoy
enjoyable
enjoyed
enjoying
enjoyment
enjoys
enormous
enough
envelope
escape
escaped
escapes
escaping
especially
evaporate
evaporated
evaporates
evaporating
even
evening
eventually
ever

every
everybody
everyone
everything
everywhere
evil
ewe
excellent
except
excite
excited
excitement
excites
exciting
expect
expected
expecting
expects
explain
explained
explaining
explains
explanation
exploration
explore
explored
explorer
explores

exploring
extinct
eye

# Ff

face
faced
faces
facing
factories
factory
fail
failed
failing
fails
failure
faint
fainted
fainting
faints
fair
fairies

| | | |
|---|---|---|
| fairy | feet | finish |
| fall | fell | finished |
| fallen | felt | finishes |
| falling | fence | finishing |
| falls | ferries | fir |
| families | ferry | fire |
| family | fête | fired |
| famous | few | fires |
| fantastic | field | fireworks |
| fare | fierce | firing |
| farm | fight | first |
| farmer | fighting | fish |
| fast | fights | fished |
| faster | figure | fishes |
| fastest | fill | fishing |
| fate | filled | five |
| father | filling | fix |
| favourite | fills | fixed |
| feast | film | fixes |
| feat | filmed | fixing |
| feather | filming | flair |
| fed | films | flame |
| feed | final | flaming |
| feeding | finally | flare |
| feeds | find | flash |
| feel | finding | flashed |
| feeling | finds | flashes |
| feels | finger | flashing |

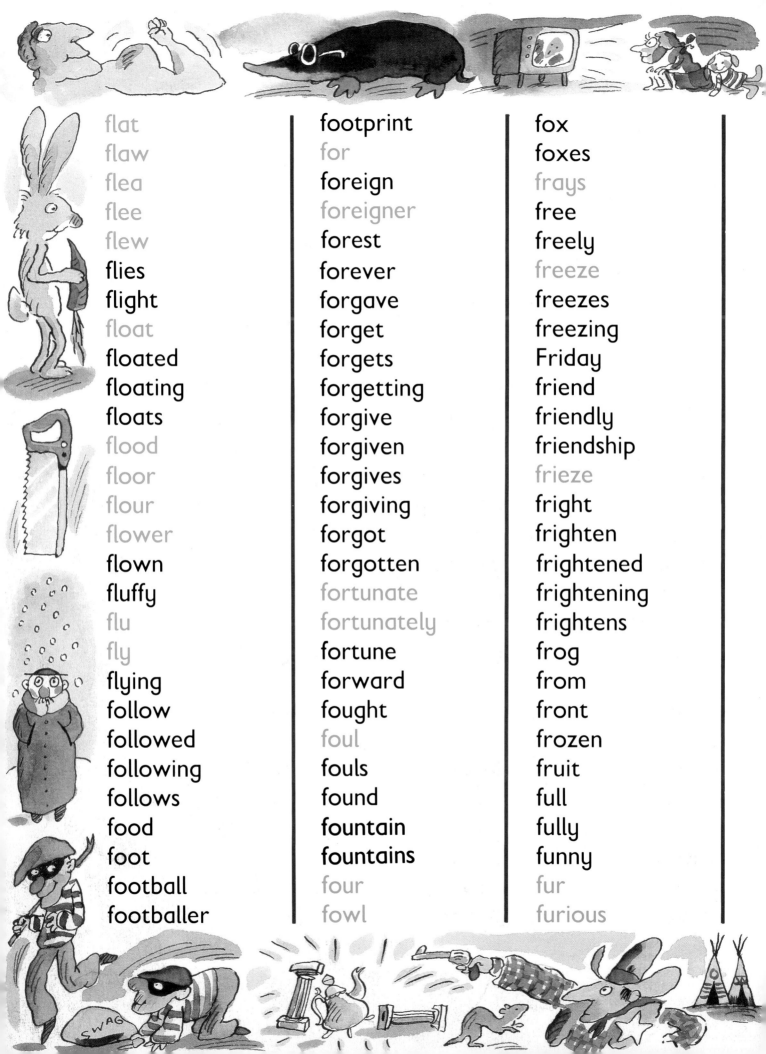

| | | |
|---|---|---|
| flat | footprint | fox |
| flaw | for | foxes |
| flea | foreign | frays |
| flee | foreigner | free |
| flew | forest | freely |
| flies | forever | freeze |
| flight | forgave | freezes |
| float | forget | freezing |
| floated | forgets | Friday |
| floating | forgetting | friend |
| floats | forgive | friendly |
| flood | forgiven | friendship |
| floor | forgives | frieze |
| flour | forgiving | fright |
| flower | forgot | frighten |
| flown | forgotten | frightened |
| fluffy | fortunate | frightening |
| flu | fortunately | frightens |
| fly | fortune | frog |
| flying | forward | from |
| follow | fought | front |
| followed | foul | frozen |
| following | fouls | fruit |
| follows | found | full |
| food | fountain | fully |
| foot | fountains | funny |
| football | four | fur |
| footballer | fowl | furious |

furiously
furry
further
future

game
gaol
garage
garden
gardener
gardening
gardens
gate
gave
geese
gerbil
get
gets
getting
ghost
giant

girl
give
given
gives
giving
glass
glasses
glue
glued
glues
gluing
gnaw
gnawed
gnawing
gnaws
gnome
go
goal
goalkeeper
goes
going
gold
golden
golf
gone
good
goodbye
goose

got
grab
grabbed
grabbing
grabs
gradual
gradually
gran
grandad
grandfather
grandma
grandmother
granny
grass
grate
great
greater
greatest
green
grew
grey
groan
groaned
groaning
groans
ground
group
grow

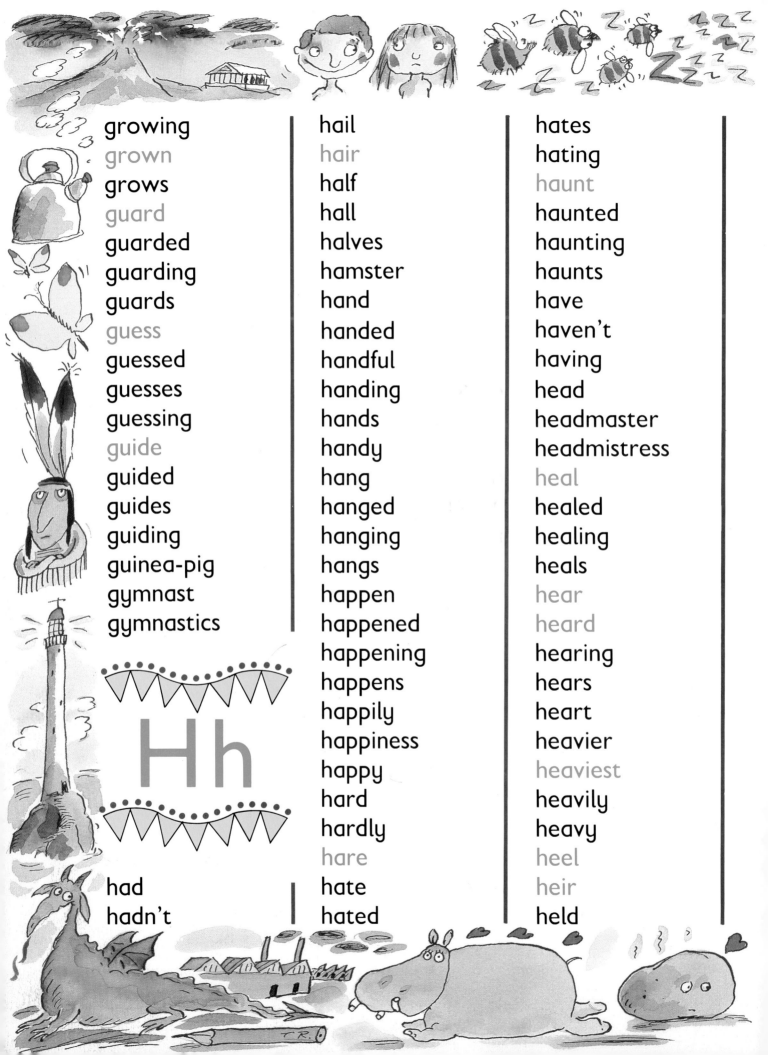

growing
grown
grows
guard
guarded
guarding
guards
guess
guessed
guesses
guessing
guide
guided
guides
guiding
guinea-pig
gymnast
gymnastics

## Hh

had
hadn't

hail
hair
half
hall
halves
hamster
hand
handed
handful
handing
hands
handy
hang
hanged
hanging
hangs
happen
happened
happening
happens
happily
happiness
happy
hard
hardly
hare
hate
hated

hates
hating
haunt
haunted
haunting
haunts
have
haven't
having
head
headmaster
headmistress
heal
healed
healing
heals
hear
heard
hearing
hears
heart
heavier
heaviest
heavily
heavy
heel
heir
held

helicopter
hello
help
helped
helping
helps
herd
here
here's
herself
hid
hidden
hide
hides
hiding
high
higher
highest
hill
him
himself
hippopotamus
hire
hired
hires
hiring
hit
hits

hitting
hoarse
hold
holding
holds
hole
holiday
hollow
home
homework
honey
hope
hoped
hopes
hoping
horn
horrible
horribly
horse
hospital
hotel
hour
house
houses
how
huge
human
humorous

humour
hundred
hung
hunger
hungry
hunt
hunted
hunting
hunts
hurried
hurries
hurry
hurrying
hurt
hurting
hurts

**I i**

I
ice-cream
I'd
idea

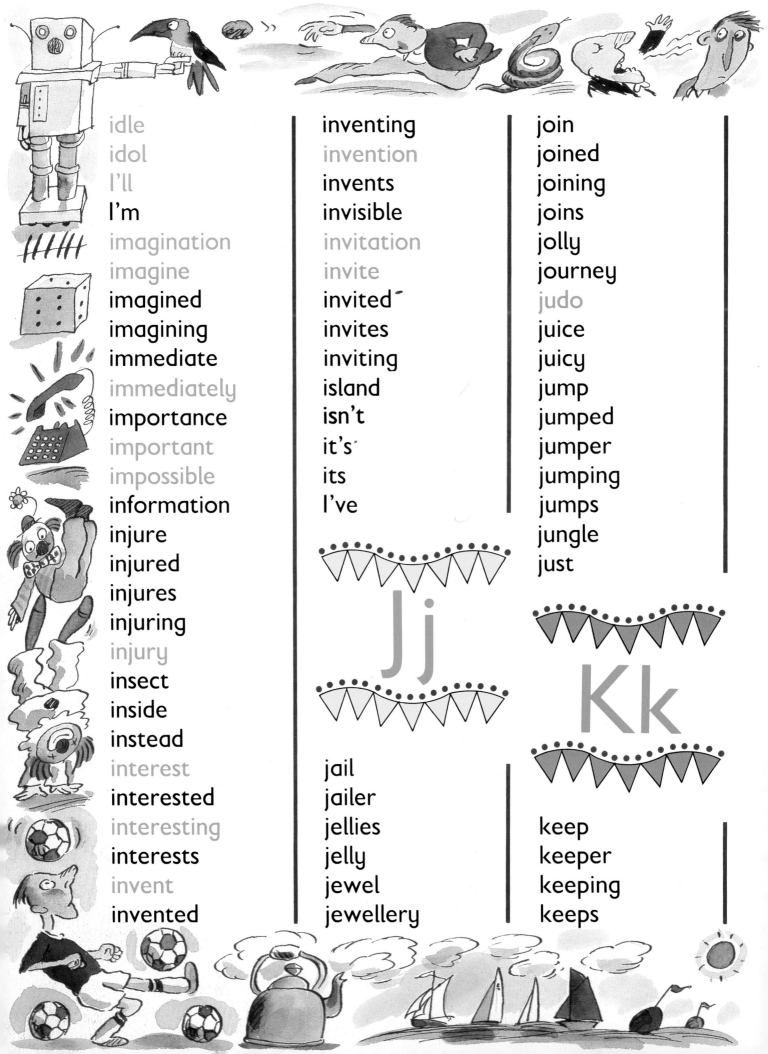

idle
idol
I'll
I'm
imagination
imagine
imagined
imagining
immediate
immediately
importance
important
impossible
information
injure
injured
injures
injuring
injury
insect
inside
instead
interest
interested
interesting
interests
invent
invented

inventing
invention
invents
invisible
invitation
invite
invited
invites
inviting
island
isn't
it's
its
I've

## Jj

jail
jailer
jellies
jelly
jewel
jewellery

join
joined
joining
joins
jolly
journey
judo
juice
juicy
jump
jumped
jumper
jumping
jumps
jungle
just

## Kk

keep
keeper
keeping
keeps

kennel
kept
kettle
key
kick
kicked
kicking
kicks
kill
killed
killer
killing
kills
kind
king
kitchen
kite
kitten
knead
knew
knife
knight
knit
knitted
knitting
knits
knives
knock

knocked
knocking
knocks
knot
know
knowing
known
knows

Ll

ladder
ladies
lady
ladybird
laid
lake
lamb
land
landed
landing
lands
lane

language
large
larger
largest
last
lasted
lasting
lasts
late
later
latest
laugh
laughed
laughing
laughs
laughter
law
lay
layer
laying
lazy
lead
leader
leading
leads
leaf
leak
leant

| | | |
|---|---|---|
| learn | lighthouse | lonely |
| learned | like | long |
| learning | liked | longer |
| learns | likes | longest |
| least | liking | look |
| leave | line | looked |
| leaves | lion | looking |
| leaving | lioness | looks |
| led | liquid | loose |
| leek | listen | lorries |
| left | listened | lorry |
| leisure | listening | lose |
| lemonade | listens | loses |
| lent | litter | losing |
| lesson | little | lost |
| let's | live | loud |
| letter | lived | lounge |
| libraries | lives | love |
| library | living | loved |
| lie | load | lovely |
| lied | loaded | loves |
| lies | loading | loving |
| life | loads | luck |
| lift | loan | luckily |
| lifted | lock | lucky |
| lifting | locked | luggage |
| lifts | locking | lunch |
| light | locks | lying |

# Mm

machine
made
magic
magical
magician
maid
mail
main
make
makes
making
male
manage
managed
manager
manages
managing
mane
manner
manor
mansion

many
mare
market
marriage
married
marries
marry
marrying
marvellous
master
match
matches
mathematics
matter
mayor
mean
meaning
means
meant
meanwhile
meat
medal
meddle
medicine
meet
meeting
meets
melt

melted
melting
melts
message
met
metal
meter
metre
mice
middle
midnight
might
mile
milk
million
mind
mine
minute
mirror
mischief
mischievous
miss
missed
misses
missing
mist
mistake
moan

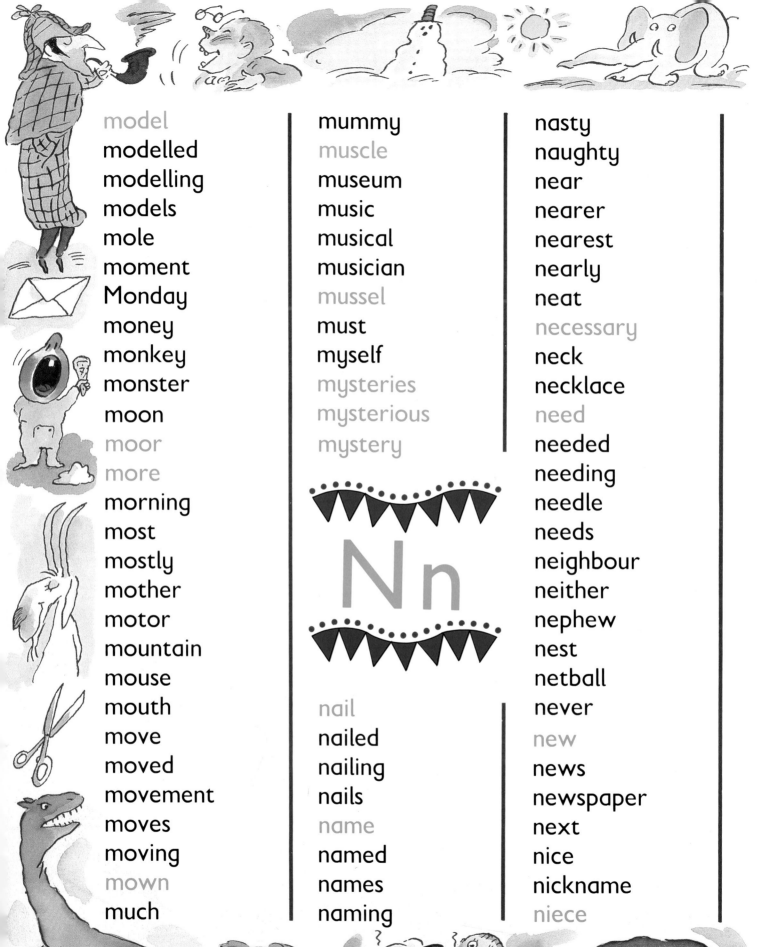

model
modelled
modelling
models
mole
moment
Monday
money
monkey
monster
moon
moor
more
morning
most
mostly
mother
motor
mountain
mouse
mouth
move
moved
movement
moves
moving
mown
much

mummy
muscle
museum
music
musical
musician
mussel
must
myself
mysteries
mysterious
mystery

# Nn

nail
nailed
nailing
nails
name
named
names
naming

nasty
naughty
near
nearer
nearest
nearly
neat
necessary
neck
necklace
need
needed
needing
needle
needs
neighbour
neither
nephew
nest
netball
never
new
news
newspaper
next
nice
nickname
niece

night
nightmare
nine
nobody
noise
noisy
none
nonsense
nor
normal
normally
nose
not
note
noted
notes
nothing
notice
noticed
notices
noticing
now
nowhere
nuisance
number
nun
nurse
nursery

# Oo

oar
object
occasion
occasionally
office
officer
o'clock
of
off
often
oil
old
older
oldest
once
one
only
open
opened
opening
opens

operation
opposite
or
orange
ordinary
ore
our
other
ourselves
outside
over
owl
own
owned
owner
owning
owns

# Pp

pack
packed
packet

packing
packs
page
paid
pain
paint
painted
painting
paints
pair
palace
pale
pancake
pane
pantomime
paper
parcel
parent
park
parked
parking
parks
parrot
parliament
part
parties
party
pass

passage
passed
passenger
passes
passing
past
pastry
patch
patched
path
patience
patient
pause
paw
paws
pay
paying
peace
peak
peal
pear
pea
pedal
pedalled
pedalling
peel
peer
penalties

penalty
pence
pencil
penny
people
person
phone
phoned
phones
phoning
photograph
phrase
pick
picked
picking
picks
picnic
picture
piece
pier
pipe
pirate
place
plaice
plain
plan
plane
planet

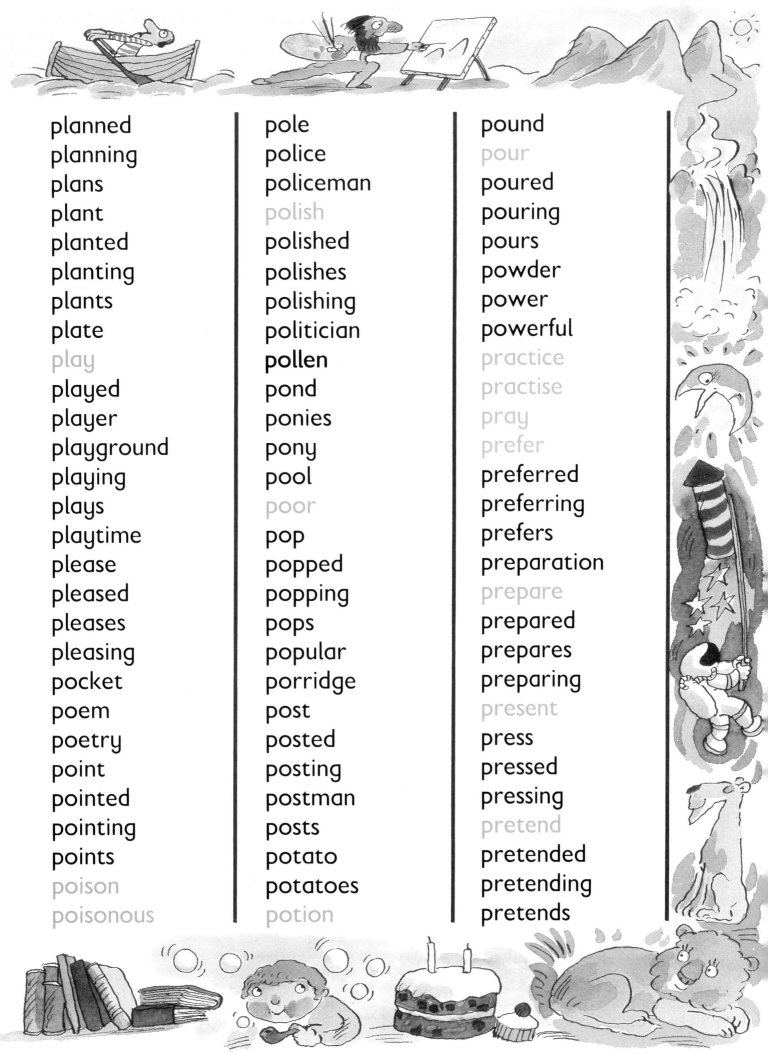

| | | |
|---|---|---|
| planned | pole | pound |
| planning | police | pour |
| plans | policeman | poured |
| plant | polish | pouring |
| planted | polished | pours |
| planting | polishes | powder |
| plants | polishing | power |
| plate | politician | powerful |
| play | pollen | practice |
| played | pond | practise |
| player | ponies | pray |
| playground | pony | prefer |
| playing | pool | preferred |
| plays | poor | preferring |
| playtime | pop | prefers |
| please | popped | preparation |
| pleased | popping | prepare |
| pleases | pops | prepared |
| pleasing | popular | prepares |
| pocket | porridge | preparing |
| poem | post | present |
| poetry | posted | press |
| point | posting | pressed |
| pointed | postman | pressing |
| pointing | posts | pretend |
| points | potato | pretended |
| poison | potatoes | pretending |
| poisonous | potion | pretends |

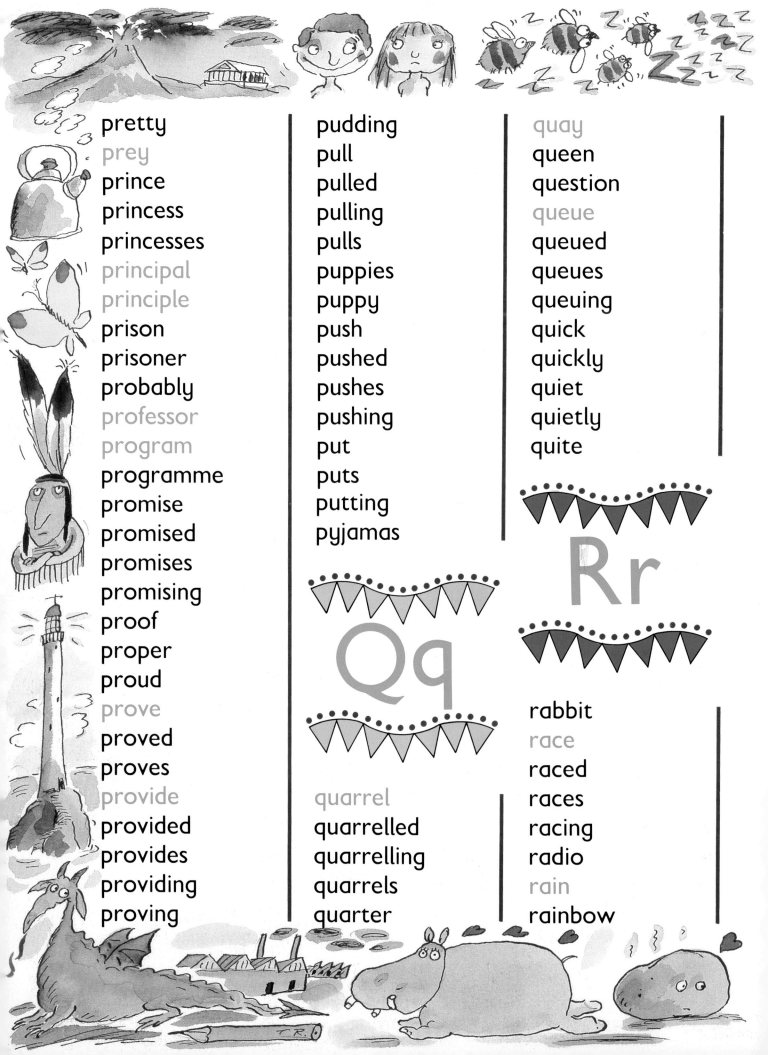

pretty
prey
prince
princess
princesses
principal
principle
prison
prisoner
probably
professor
program
programme
promise
promised
promises
promising
proof
proper
proud
prove
proved
proves
provide
provided
provides
providing
proving

pudding
pull
pulled
pulling
pulls
puppies
puppy
push
pushed
pushes
pushing
put
puts
putting
pyjamas

quay
queen
question
queue
queued
queues
queuing
quick
quickly
quiet
quietly
quite

# Qq

quarrel
quarrelled
quarrelling
quarrels
quarter

# Rr

rabbit
race
raced
races
racing
radio
rain
rainbow

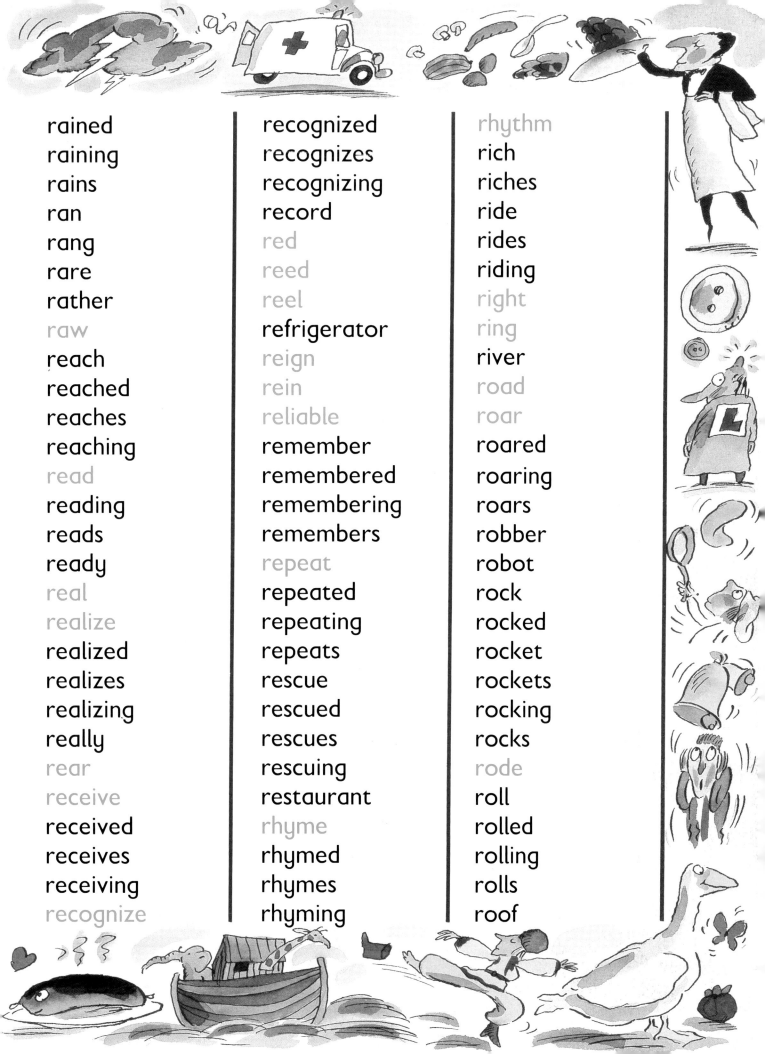

| | | |
|---|---|---|
| rained | recognized | rhythm |
| raining | recognizes | rich |
| rains | recognizing | riches |
| ran | record | ride |
| rang | red | rides |
| rare | reed | riding |
| rather | reel | right |
| raw | refrigerator | ring |
| reach | reign | river |
| reached | rein | road |
| reaches | reliable | roar |
| reaching | remember | roared |
| read | remembered | roaring |
| reading | remembering | roars |
| reads | remembers | robber |
| ready | repeat | robot |
| real | repeated | rock |
| realize | repeating | rocked |
| realized | repeats | rocket |
| realizes | rescue | rockets |
| realizing | rescued | rocking |
| really | rescues | rocks |
| rear | rescuing | rode |
| receive | restaurant | roll |
| received | rhyme | rolled |
| receives | rhymed | rolling |
| receiving | rhymes | rolls |
| recognize | rhyming | roof |

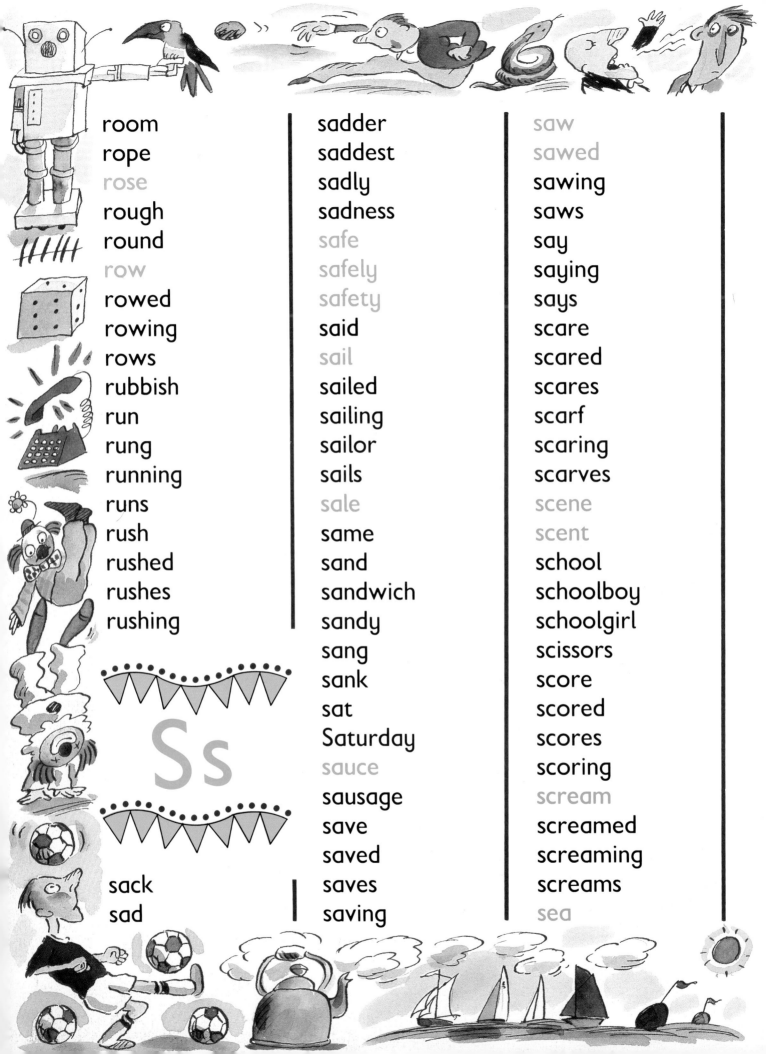

room
rope
rose
rough
round
row
rowed
rowing
rows
rubbish
run
rung
running
runs
rush
rushed
rushes
rushing

sack
sad

**Ss**

sadder
saddest
sadly
sadness
safe
safely
safety
said
sail
sailed
sailing
sailor
sails
sale
same
sand
sandwich
sandy
sang
sank
sat
Saturday
sauce
sausage
save
saved
saves
saving

saw
sawed
sawing
saws
say
saying
says
scare
scared
scares
scarf
scaring
scarves
scene
scent
school
schoolboy
schoolgirl
scissors
score
scored
scores
scoring
scream
screamed
screaming
screams
sea

| | | | |
|---|---|---|---|
| seal | sell | shall |  |
| sealed | seller | shape | |
| sealing | selling | shaped | |
| seals | sells | shapes | |
| seam | send | shaping | |
| search | sending | share | |
| searched | sends | shared | |
| searches | sense | shares | |
| searching | sent | sharing | |
| seas | sentence | shark | |
| seaside | separate | sharp | |
| second | separated | shear |  |
| secret | separates | sheared | |
| see | separating | shearing | |
| seed | serial | shears | |
| seeds | serious | sheep | |
| seeing | seriously | sheer | |
| seem | servant | shelf | |
| seemed | seven | shell | |
| seeming | severe | shelves | |
| seems | sew | sheriff | |
| seen | sewed | shield | |
| sees | sewing | shine | |
| seize | sewn | shining | |
| seized | sews | ship | |
| seizes | shadow | shoe | |
| seizing | shake | shone | |
| selfish | shaking | shook | |

| | | |
|---|---|---|
| shoot | sickness | skipped |
| shooting | side | skipping |
| shoots | sight | skips |
| shop | sign | skirt |
| shopped | silence | sky |
| shopping | silly | sledge |
| shops | silver | sledging |
| shore | since | sleep |
| short | sincerely | sleeping |
| shot | sing | sleeps |
| should | singing | sleigh |
| shoulder | sings | slept |
| shout | sink | slid |
| shouted | sinking | slide |
| shouting | sinks | sliding |
| shouts | sister | slip |
| show | sit | slipped |
| showed | site | slippery |
| showing | sits | slipping |
| shows | sitting | slips |
| shrank | six | slow |
| shrink | sixty | slowly |
| shrinking | size | slows |
| shrinks | skate | small |
| shut | skated | smaller |
| shuts | skates | smallest |
| shutting | skating | smash |
| sick | skip | smashed |

smashes
smashing
smell
smelling
smells
smelly
smelt
smile
smiled
smiles
smiling
smoke
smoked
smokes
smoking
snake
snooker
snow
snowball
snowed
snowing
snowman
snows
so
soar
soared
soaring
soars

sock
soft
softer
softest
softly
sold
soldier
some
somebody
someone
something
sometimes
somewhere
son
song
soon
sore
sorry
sort
sorted
sorting
sorts
sound
sounded
sounding
sounds
soup
sour

source
sow
space
spaceship
spade
spare
speak
speaking
speaks
spear
special
speed
spell
spend
spending
spends
spent
spider
spin
spinning
spins
spirit
spoke
spoken
spoon
sport
spot
spots

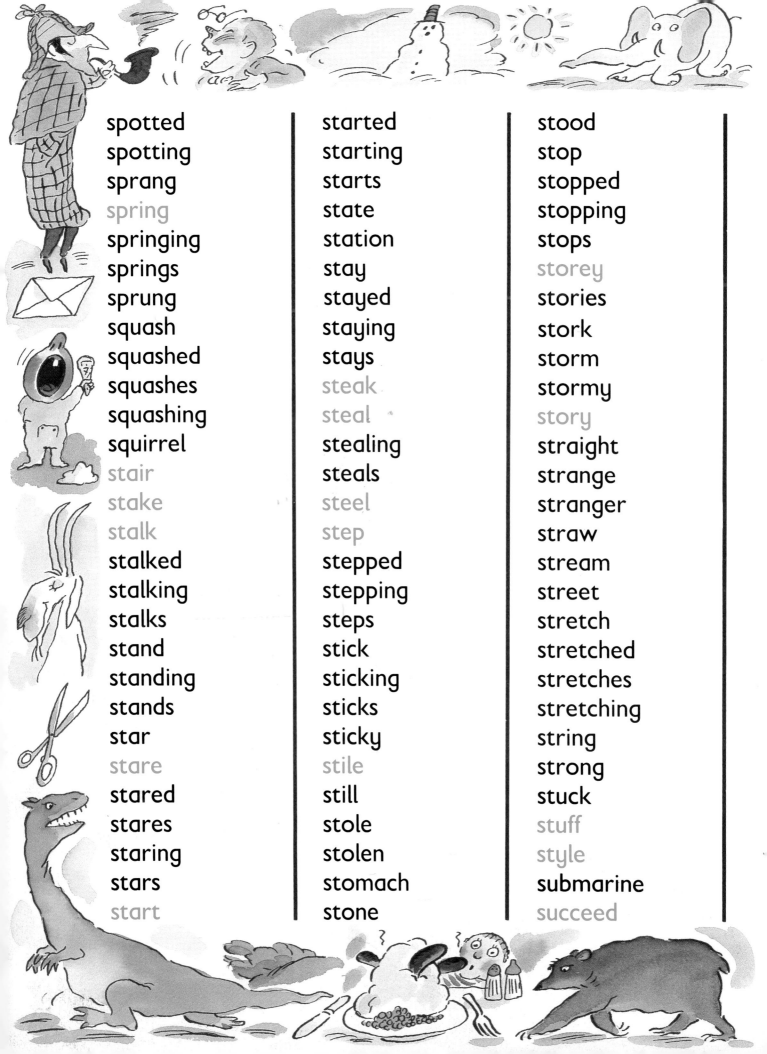

| | | |
|---|---|---|
| spotted | started | stood |
| spotting | starting | stop |
| sprang | starts | stopped |
| spring | state | stopping |
| springing | station | stops |
| springs | stay | storey |
| sprung | stayed | stories |
| squash | staying | stork |
| squashed | stays | storm |
| squashes | steak | stormy |
| squashing | steal | story |
| squirrel | stealing | straight |
| stair | steals | strange |
| stake | steel | stranger |
| stalk | step | straw |
| stalked | stepped | stream |
| stalking | stepping | street |
| stalks | steps | stretch |
| stand | stick | stretched |
| standing | sticking | stretches |
| stands | sticks | stretching |
| star | sticky | string |
| stare | stile | strong |
| stared | still | stuck |
| stares | stole | stuff |
| staring | stolen | style |
| stars | stomach | submarine |
| start | stone | succeed |

succeeded
succeeding
succeeds
success
sudden
suddenly
sugar
suite
sum
summer
sun
Sunday
sung
sunk
sunny
sunshine
super
supper
sure
surprise
surprised
surprises
surprising
swam
swan
sweet
swim
swimming

swims
swing
swinging
swings
switch
switched
switches
switching
sword
swum
swung

# Tt

table
tadpole
tail
take
taken
takes
taking
tale
talk

talked
talking
talks
tall
taller
tallest
taught
tea
teach
teacher
teaches
teaching
team
teddies
teddy
teeth
telephone
television
tell
telling
tells
temple
tent
terrible
test
tested
testing
tests

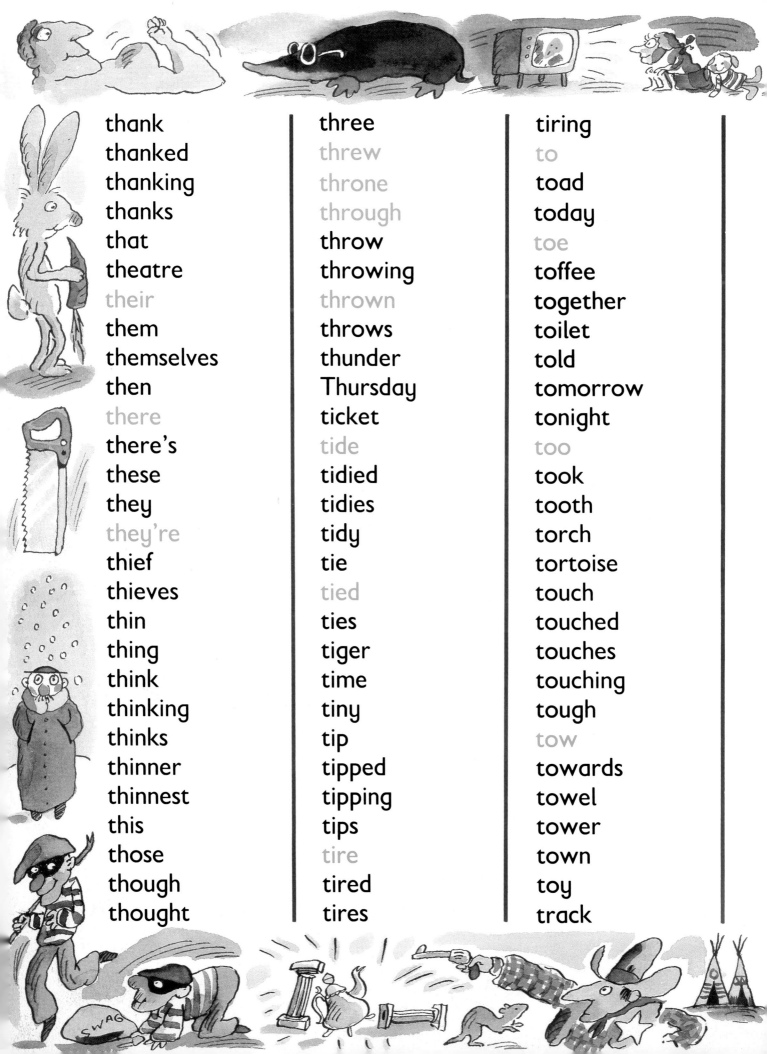

| | | |
|---|---|---|
| thank | three | tiring |
| thanked | threw | to |
| thanking | throne | toad |
| thanks | through | today |
| that | throw | toe |
| theatre | throwing | toffee |
| their | thrown | together |
| them | throws | toilet |
| themselves | thunder | told |
| then | Thursday | tomorrow |
| there | ticket | tonight |
| there's | tide | too |
| these | tidied | took |
| they | tidies | tooth |
| they're | tidy | torch |
| thief | tie | tortoise |
| thieves | tied | touch |
| thin | ties | touched |
| thing | tiger | touches |
| think | time | touching |
| thinking | tiny | tough |
| thinks | tip | tow |
| thinner | tipped | towards |
| thinnest | tipping | towel |
| this | tips | tower |
| those | tire | town |
| though | tired | toy |
| thought | tires | track |

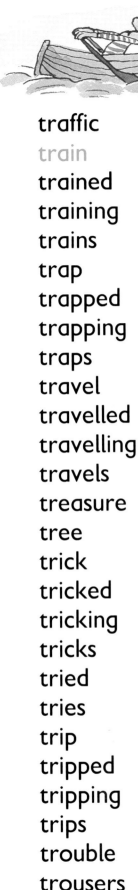

traffic
train
trained
training
trains
trap
trapped
trapping
traps
travel
travelled
travelling
travels
treasure
tree
trick
tricked
tricking
tricks
tried
tries
trip
tripped
tripping
trips
trouble
trousers
true

try
trying
Tuesday
tunnel
turn
turned
turning
turns
tying
twelve
twenty
two
tyre

## Uu

uglier
ugliest
ugly
umbrella
uncle
under
underground

underneath
understand
understanding
understands
understood
unhappy
until
upon
upstairs
use
used
uses
using
usually

## Vv

vain
vanish
vanished
vanishes
vanishing
vegetable

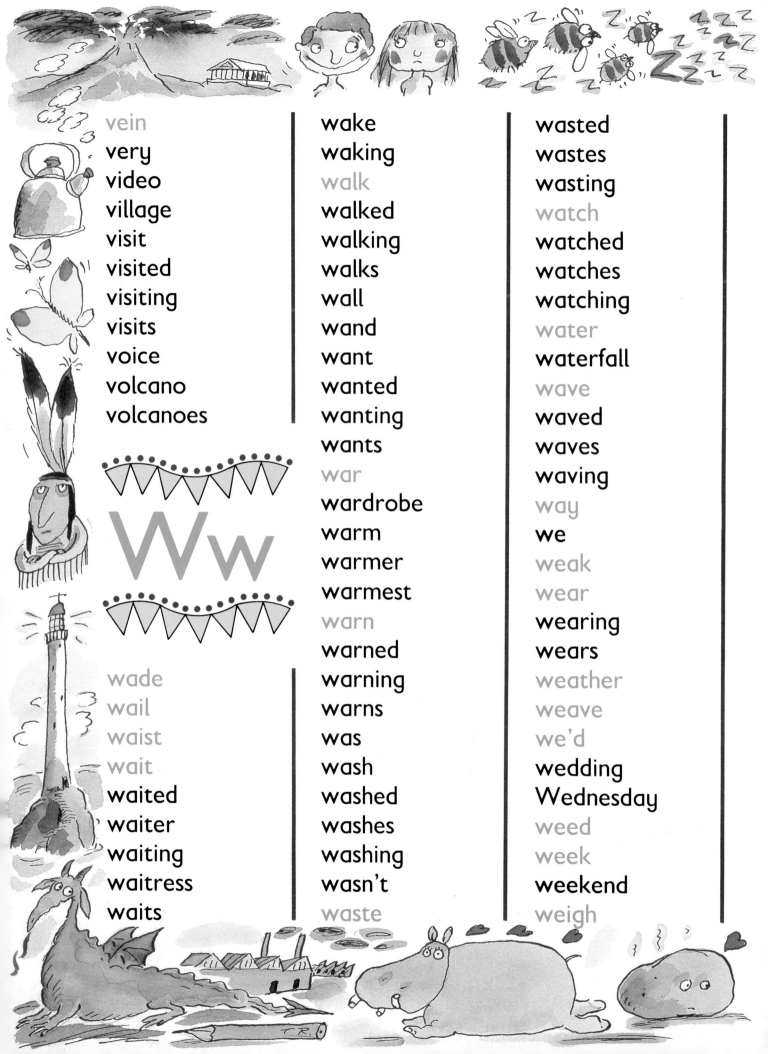

vein
very
video
village
visit
visited
visiting
visits
voice
volcano
volcanoes

# Ww

wade
wail
waist
wait
waited
waiter
waiting
waitress
waits

wake
waking
walk
walked
walking
walks
wall
wand
want
wanted
wanting
wants
war
wardrobe
warm
warmer
warmest
warn
warned
warning
warns
was
wash
washed
washes
washing
wasn't
waste

wasted
wastes
wasting
watch
watched
watches
watching
water
waterfall
wave
waved
waves
waving
way
we
weak
wear
wearing
wears
weather
weave
we'd
wedding
Wednesday
weed
week
weekend
weigh

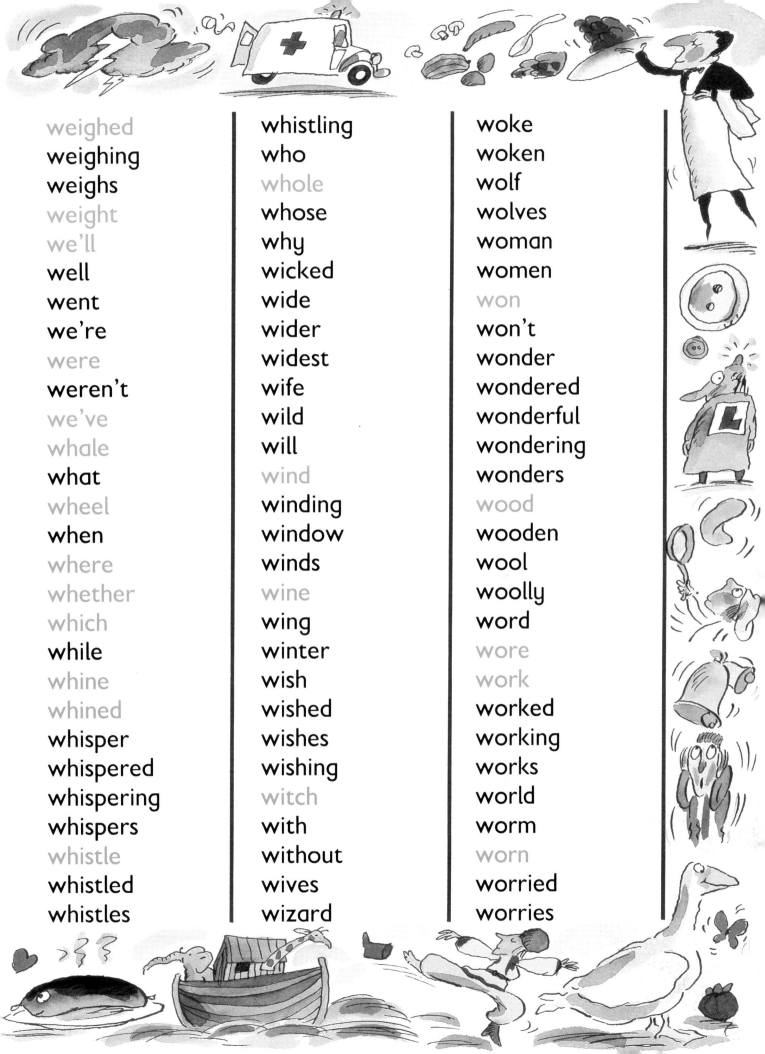

weighed
weighing
weighs
weight
we'll
well
went
we're
were
weren't
we've
whale
what
wheel
when
where
whether
which
while
whine
whined
whisper
whispered
whispering
whispers
whistle
whistled
whistles

whistling
who
whole
whose
why
wicked
wide
wider
widest
wife
wild
will
wind
winding
window
winds
wine
wing
winter
wish
wished
wishes
wishing
witch
with
without
wives
wizard

woke
woken
wolf
wolves
woman
women
won
won't
wonder
wondered
wonderful
wondering
wonders
wood
wooden
wool
woolly
word
wore
work
worked
working
works
world
worm
worn
worried
worries

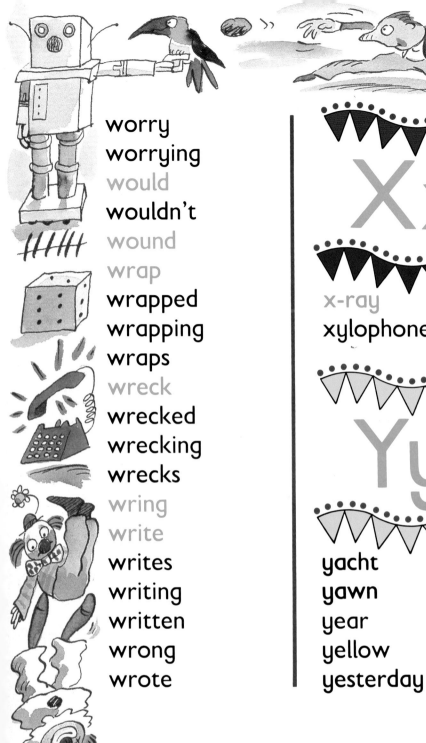

worry
worrying
would
wouldn't
wound
wrap
wrapped
wrapping
wraps
wreck
wrecked
wrecking
wrecks
wring
write
writes
writing
written
wrong
wrote

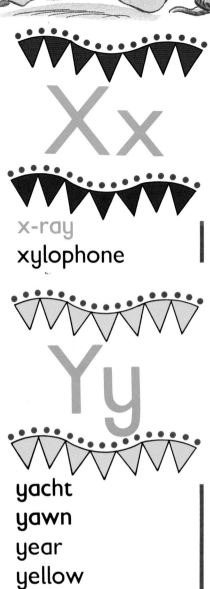

## Xx

x-ray
xylophone

## Yy

yacht
yawn
year
yellow
yesterday

yoghurt
yoke
yolk
you
you'll
you're
you've
young
younger
youngest
your

## Zz

zebra
zoo

# Definition Dictionary

This part of the dictionary is designed to help your child use words correctly.

▷ words are listed in alphabetical order

▷ each word is used in a sentence which makes its meaning clear

▷ words in brackets indicate pronunciation guide

Some words may be confusing to a child because

▷ the word may sound exactly like another word (e.g. bear/bare)

▷ we may sometimes use the word as a noun (e.g. I read this **book**) and sometimes as a verb (e.g. Please **book** the cinema tickets)

▷ or the word may present difficulties for some other reason and your child would benefit from seeing the word used accurately in a sentence

For these reasons, some of the words in the *Spelling Dictionary* (pages 3–42) also appear in this special *Definition Dictionary*. (These words are printed in blue in the *Spelling Dictionary*.)

In this *Definition Dictionary* you will see some words have another following it in brackets. These are to guide your child on the correct pronunciation of the word (e.g. after the word "bass" is the clue, "rhymes with face"). Explain this to your child so he or she can become familiar with the conventions of this dictionary.

All the words listed in this section also appear printed in blue in the *Spelling Dictionary*.

# Aa

## accept
I **accepted** the sweet my friend gave me and ate it quickly.

## achieve
She'd always wanted to fly an aeroplane and this year she **achieved** her dream.

## address
1 Danny Smith's **address** is 27 Broad Street.

2 I **addressed** the envelope to Danny. ▼

## admiration
We showed our **admiration** by clapping and cheering.

## admire
Wayne **admired** Daley Thompson very much. He hoped that one day he would be a great sportsman too.

## admit
1 This ticket **admits** you to the pop concert.

2 The thief **admitted** that he took the watch.

## advertise
John wanted to sell his bike. "Why don't you **advertise** it in the paper?" said Mum.

## advertisement
I saw the **advertisement** on television and decided to buy these biscuits. ▼

## advice
She gave us good **advice** when she told us to come here.

## advise
The policewoman said, "I **advise** you to cross at the zebra crossing."

## aerial
An **aerial** is a rod or wire which receives or sends out television or radio waves. ▼

**affect**
The change of the bus timetable will **affect** us all.

**air**
1    I opened the window and breathed in the fresh **air**.
2    Andrew felt there was an **air** of mystery in the room.
3    They put out the clothes to **air** in the sun.

**allowed**
Simon is 10 so he's **allowed** to stay up late.

**aloud**
Jaswinder read her poem **aloud** to the class.

**altar**
The light streamed through the church window and on to the **altar**. ▾

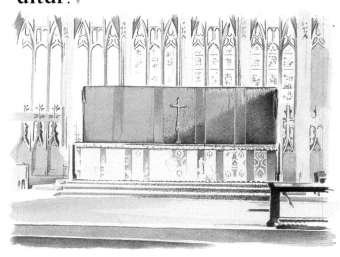

**alter**
When he made a slight mistake in his writing, the teacher said, "Don't bother to **alter** it."

**although**
We went for a walk **although** it was pouring with rain.

**amaze**
Our class was **amazed** when we won the cup. We thought we wouldn't do very well.

**amazing**
She was wearing such an **amazing** dress that everyone stared at her.

**annoy**
You **annoy** other people if you shout when they want to be quiet.

**answer**
1    Do you know the **answer** to the next question?
2    Rosa, will you **answer** the question?

**anxiety**
We waited with **anxiety** for news that he had arrived safely. We were very worried.

**anxious**
1    Catherine is **anxious** about her exam results because she doesn't think she's done well.
2    Ravi is **anxious** to be a member of the team.

**anxiously**
Amy looked around **anxiously**. She did not know where she was.

45

**apologize**
You must **apologize** to Jaswart for breaking his bike.

**apology**
I accepted her **apology** and forgave her.

**appear**
1 At last the car **appeared** at the top of the hill. ▼

2 What she said **appears** to be true so we must believe her.
3 Liam **appeared** in a TV film about our town.

**appearance**
1 Paul's sudden **appearance** in the room surprised us.
2 His **appearance** was very strange. He had green hair and he wore odd clothes.

**are**
We **are** going shopping today.

**aren't**
They **aren't** going shopping, they're staying at home.

**argue**
Beth and David **argue** about whose turn it is to set the table.

**argument**
Sue and Ramu had an **argument** about who should have the last cake.

**arrange**
Mr Fletcher **arranged** for our class to go to the seaside.

**arrangement**
Mum had made a beautiful **arrangement** of flowers. ▼

**artificial**
The **artificial** flowers were made of silk.

**assist**
You **assist** someone when you help them to do something.

**assistance**

Old Mrs Carr needs some **assistance** to climb the stairs.

**astonish**

I was **astonished** I won the painting competition. I didn't think my picture was that good.

**astonishment**

To my **astonishment**, the bird flew right on to my hand.

**ate**

Jim **ate** an egg for breakfast.

**attention**

1   Pay careful **attention** and you will understand this difficult story.

2   The soldiers stood to **attention** with their feet together and staring straight ahead. ▾

**aunt**

Your **aunt** is your mother's or father's sister.

**avoid**

You can **avoid** the traffic by going down this quiet road.

**balance**

1   We used a **balance** to weigh the sugar.

2   Fraser **balanced** the book on his head as he walked. ▾

**ball**

1   The children kicked the **ball** across the grass.

2   Cinderella danced at the **ball** until midnight. ▾

## bare

1  Sharon loved walking in the rain in **bare** feet.

2  The room was **bare**. There was no furniture in it.

3  The dog **bared** its teeth at the stranger. ▼

## bargain

1  We made a **bargain**. If I worked hard, Dad would take me to the fun-fair.

2  It was a real **bargain**. It usually costs £1 and I bought it for 25p.

## base

The climbers headed back to **base** camp. ▼

## bass (rhymes with face)

A **bass** singer has a deep, low voice.

## beach

We ran down the sandy **beach** to the sea. ▼

## bean

There was only one baked **bean** left on his plate.

## bear

1  A huge **bear** rushed out of the forest. ▼

2  I can't **bear** watching horror films.

### beech
A copper **beech** is a tree with beautiful reddy-brown leaves. ▼

### been
I went shopping yesterday. Have you **been** to the shops?

### beginner
As I am only a **beginner**, I can't play tennis very well.

### beginning
Let's start at the **beginning** of the story, not the end.

### believe
I **believe** you're telling the truth.

### berry
The holly **berry** is bright red.

### bite
You'll break your teeth if you **bite** that nut.

### blew
The wind **blew** hard all day.

### blue
It was a lovely day with a clear **blue** sky.

### board
1   Alex pinned his notice on the **board**. ▼

2   The floor was made of thin **boards** of polished wood.

3   They called our names when it was time to **board** the plane.

### boast
1   Hugh is always **boasting**. He says he is bigger and cleverer than anyone else.

2   It is her **boast** that she can run faster than Carl.

### boastful
Hugh is very **boastful**. He's always telling us how clever he is.

### bold
You'd have to be a **bold** person to dare to ride that wild horse!

### bolder
She must be **bolder** than me if she dares to ride that wild horse.

### book
1   This dictionary is a **book**.

2   Please **book** three tickets on the coach.

## bored

1 He had heard the story three times already and was **bored** by it.

2 Dave **bored** a hole in the wall to see through.

## bough

There was a swing hanging from a **bough** of the tree.▾

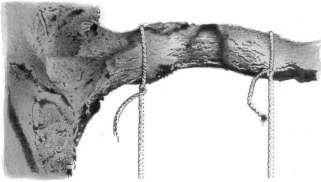

## boulder

After the landslide, a huge **boulder** blocked the path.

## bow (rhymes with cow)

1 The girls curtsy and the boys **bow** to the prince.

2 The **bow** is the front part of a ship.▾

## bow (rhymes with go)

1 Kamla wore a red **bow** in her hair.

2 She got a **bow** and arrow for her birthday.

## bowled

Gopal **bowled** Angus out with the first ball of the cricket match.

## boy

There were seven girls and four **boys** in the team.

## brake

1 The **brake** on a bicycle makes it slow down or stop.

2 A car must **brake** when it reaches a crossroads.

## break

1 The glass will **break** if you drop it.

2 We played marbles during **break**.

## breath

Hold your **breath** when you swim under water.

## breathe

If you **breathe** in deeply you will smell the sea.

## bridge

1 We crossed the river by a wooden **bridge**.

2 **Bridge** is a game of cards.

## buoy

A **buoy** is a marker to show sailors where it is safe to sail. ▼

## burrow

1   Rabbits dig a **burrow** in the ground to live in. ▼

2   Lisa's dog **burrowed** into the sand and found a bone.

## bury

Our dog likes to **bury** his bone in the flower-bed.

## busily

The girl was **busily** painting and didn't see me.

## business

1   My aunt is in the tourist **business**. She arranges holidays.

2   Mind your own **business**. It's nothing to do with you.

## buy

We go to the baker to **buy** bread.

## by

1   The goal was scored **by** Tina.

2   Try to get here **by** 3.30pm.

3   There is a lamp **by** my bed.

## byte

A **byte** is a group of eight bits that belong together to make one unit in a computer.

## calculator

I'm going to use my **calculator** to do this sum.

## calendar

A **calendar** shows the days of the week and the months of the year.

## capsize

Our boat **capsized** and we fell into the water. ▼

**careless**
Helen was **careless** and so she made many mistakes.

**caught**
Clare **caught** the ball when it was thrown to her.

**ceiling**
Deborah lay on her bed and looked up at the **ceiling**.

**cell**
1   A **cell** is one tiny part of a living thing.▼

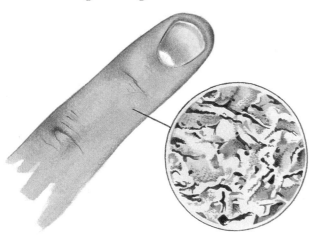

2   The prisoner spent the night in a **cell** at the police station.

**cellar**
We went down the steps into the **cellar** below the house.

**cemetery**
The old man died and was buried in the **cemetery**.

**century** (means 100)
1   My grandfather was born in 1880, over a **century** ago.

2   Lloyd scored a **century** at cricket last week.▼

**cereal**
My favourite **cereal** is cornflakes.

**certain**
1   Are you **certain** that this is your pen?

2   Shirley wanted a **certain** watch. She did not want any other one.

**certainly**
That plant will **certainly** die if you don't water it.

**character**
My favourite **character** in the play is Mr Toad.

**check**
1   I always **check** that the water for the birds has not frozen in winter.

2   Jaswinder wore a black and red **check** skirt and a plain red shirt.

**cheer**

1 Our class gave a great **cheer** when we heard that our team had won.

2 We all **cheer** loudly at football matches.

**cheque**

Mum paid the bill with a **cheque** from her cheque-book.

**choice**

There is a **choice**. We can have lemonade or orange squash.

**chord**

Play a **chord** on the piano.

**chute** (say shoot)

We slid down the **chute** into the water. ▼

**coach**

1 We have a football **coach** who trains our team.

2 Natasha **coached** the team for the competition.

3 We travelled in a **coach** to the seaside.

4 The boys all got into the same **coach** on the train.

5 Cinderella's **coach** turned into a pumpkin at midnight.

**coarse**

This jumper is made of such **coarse** wool it makes me itch.

**collect**

1 Let's **collect** conkers from under that tree.

2 Manjit **collects** stamps and puts them in his stamp album.

**collection**

1 Manjit has a fine **collection** of stamps.

2 We had a **collection** at school and it added up to £50.

**collide**

The van **collided** with the car on the slippery road.

**collision**

There was a **collision** between a van and a car, but no one was hurt. ▼

**comfortable**

These shoes are so **comfortable** that I like to wear them all the time.

**compare**

Try to **compare** these two stories. Which do you think is the better one?

**comparison**

We made a **comparison** between the two pictures and then we saw the differences.

**complain**

Stephen **complained** that his new shoes were too tight.

**complaint**

Emma made a **complaint** about the bus service and they tried to improve it.

**cook**

1   Hasina learned how to **cook** vegetables.▼

2   The **cook** made curry for dinner today.

**cord**

Tie the parcels together with this piece of **cord**.

**correct**

1   Your work is **correct**. You didn't make any mistakes.

2   This is the **correct** way to do it.

**correction**

When Ann got a sum wrong, she had to make a **correction**.

**course**

1   Of **course** I want to come.

2   The boat stayed on its **course** across the lake.

3   The horses raced down the **course** to the winning post.▼

**court**

1   The tennis **court** was marked out with white lines.

2   Peter had to go to **court** to explain how the car accident had happened.

3   We were invited to **court** to meet the king.

**create**

You **create** something when you make something no one has made before.

**creation**

I've made an amazing **creation** with my modelling clay.

**cross**

1 I **cross** a busy road on my way to school.

2 I couldn't read it because it was **crossed** out.

3 Dad was very **cross** with me when I broke his pen.

4 We made a **cross** with two bits of wood.

**crown**

1 The king wore a beautiful golden **crown** on his head.

2 Elizabeth II was **crowned** Queen of England in 1953.

**cruel**

It's **cruel** to tease the kitten.

**cruelty**

You know that **cruelty** to animals is against the law.

**crystal**

A **crystal** looks like a bit of glass.▼

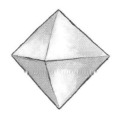

**cue**

The actor came on stage when he heard his **cue**.

**currant**

We have a red **currant** bush in our garden.

**current**

The lights stop working when the electric **current** is switched off.

**customer**

A person who uses a shop or bank is a **customer** of that place.

Dd

**damage**

1 The storm **damaged** the roof and Dad had to replace the tiles.

2 Mum and Dad repaired the **damage** done by the storm.▼

55

**dangerous**
It is **dangerous** to play near a busy road.

**dangerously**
They stood **dangerously** near the edge of the cliff.

**dare**
1 I never **dare** walk along the wall because it's too high.
2 I **dare** you to do it.

**dear**
1 "Come along, **dear**," Dad said. "It's time to go."
2 Dad couldn't afford it because it was too **dear**.

**decide**
Can you **decide** what you want?

**decision**
It was a difficult **decision** but in the end I chose the blue jeans not the black ones.

**deer**
Male **deer** have antlers. ▼

**definition**
The **definition** of a word is what the word means.

**delay**
1 The rain **delayed** us and made us late.
2 Because of the **delay**, we arrived two hours late.

**deliberate**
The teacher made a **deliberate** mistake and then asked the class if they could say what she had done wrong.

**deliberately**
I was cross. She was being **deliberately** annoying.

**deny**
Don't **deny** it! I know you did it.

**depend**
1 The blind man **depends** on the help of his guide-dog to walk in the street.
2 It all **depends** on the weather. We may not be able to go.

**desert** (say dez-ert)
There is little rain in a **desert** and the ground is very sandy. ▼

**desert** (say de-zert)
When he was in trouble his friends **deserted** him.

**dessert** (say de-zert)
We had ice-cream for **dessert**.

**destroy**
The wind and rain **destroyed** the prize-winning roses.

**destruction**
The earthquake left terrible **destruction** in the town. Many people lost their homes.

**dew**
The grass is wet with **dew** in the early morning. ▼

**die**
The flowers will **die** if you don't put them in water.

**died**
When my dog **died** I was very unhappy.

**difference**
Can you spot the **differences** between these two pictures? ▼

**different**
She tried five **different** sorts of shoes but didn't like any of them.

## direct
The police officer **directed** the cars away from the accident. ▼

## direction
In which **direction** is the wind blowing – north or west?

## disappear
One moment he was there and the next he wasn't. He had completely **disappeared**.

## disappoint
Jan was **disappointed** that she missed the film.

## disappointment
When he lost the race, Anthony cried with **disappointment**.

## discover
1   Sanjay **discovered** an old coin in the desk drawer.

2   We **discovered** that it was too late to catch the plane.

## disguise (say dis-gise)
1   They used funny masks as a **disguise**.

2   The children **disguised** themselves with masks.

## divide
If you **divide** 10 by 2, the answer is 5.

## division
1   Everton have been in the first **division** for years.

2   Can you do this long **division** sum?   29$\overline{)406}$

## doe
A female deer or a female rabbit is called a **doe**. ▼

## dormitory
At boarding school I sleep in a **dormitory** with six other girls.

## dough
You use **dough** to make bread and doughnuts. It is a mixture of flour and water.

## draw
1   Can you **draw** a circle with your pencil?

2   The match was a **draw**. The score was two points for each team.

## drawer

Ivan discovered a secret **drawer** in his desk. ▼

## dream

1   Last night when I was asleep I had a **dream** that I was an astronaut.

2   Hugh **dreamed** that he was a pilot.

3   My **dream** is that one day I will be a disc jockey.

## drive

1   Can you **drive** the lorry to the factory?

2   Let's go for a **drive** in your new car.

3   A long **drive** led from the gate up to the house.

## due

1   My book is **due** back at the library today.

2   The accident was **due** to the icy roads.

## dungeon

The prisoner was kept in a **dungeon** in the castle. ▼

## dye

He coloured his hair red with the **dye**.

## dyed

I **dyed** my shirt blue to match my jeans.

## ear

1   I hear with my **ears** and see with my eyes.

2   The seeds at the top of a stalk of corn are called the **ears**.

## edge

1   The ball rolled to the **edge** of the table. She caught it before it fell off.

2   At the scary bit of the film, I **edged** closer to Mum.

## effect

The **effect** of the rain was to make the path muddy.

**eight**
I'm seven. Soon I'll be **eight**.

**employer**
Your **employer** is the person you work for.

**emptied**
Frank **emptied** all the water out of the bucket.

**empty**
Everyone had gone and the room was **empty**.

**evaporate**
Water **evaporates** when it is heated and changes from liquid to steam. ▼

**excellent**
Mum was very pleased with my **excellent** school report.

**except**
Everyone got a prize **except** Mark who had done badly.

**excitement**
The little children jumped up and down with **excitement** when Father Christmas arrived.

**explain**
Please **explain** how this machine works.

**explanation**
Her **explanation** was so good that we knew exactly what to do.

**exploration**
The **exploration** of outer space is a very exciting adventure.

**explore**
We **explored** the country all around the camp.

**fail**
Ben tried very hard but he **failed** to swim 10 lengths.

**failure**
Ben was very disappointed by his **failure** to swim 10 lengths.

**faint**
1  He felt **faint** and dizzy after standing for an hour.
2  She drew it **faintly** in pencil and then went over it in pen.

**fair**
1  All the children had a **fair** share of the cake.
2  Robert's hair is **fair** and his eyes are blue.
3  We hope we'll have **fair** weather for sports day.

4 Tony enjoyed the big wheel best of all the rides at the **fair**. ▾

**fare**

Children don't have to pay the full **fare** on buses and trains.

**fate**

The **fate** of the prisoner will be decided by the judge.

**feat**

It was a remarkable **feat** to win three races.

**feet**

1 Ducks have webbed **feet**.

2 The giant was 11 **feet** tall.

**ferry**

1 Can you **ferry** me across the river in your boat?

2 We went across the channel by **ferry**. ▾

**fête**

There were lots of stalls at the **fête**. There were races and games too.

**film**

1 We went to the cinema and saw a **film** about pirates.

2 You need **film** in your camera to take photographs.

3 When the rhino charged, Nick **filmed** all the action with his camera. ▾

4 There was a thin **film** of oil on the water.

## fir
**Fir** trees stay green even during winter. ▼

## fish
1 A **fish** has fins and gills so it can live and breathe in water.
2 Alan likes **fishing** in this pond.

## flair
Sita had a **flair** for sport. She was particularly good at tennis.

## flare
The fire will **flare** up if you put more wood on it.

## flash
1 You use a **flash** to take photographs in the dark.
2 There was a news **flash** about the accident.
3 The lighthouse light **flashes** once a minute.

4 There was a **flash** of lightning; then a roll of thunder. ▼

## flat
1 I live in a **flat** on the second floor of that house.
2 If you are drawing a picture, you need a **flat** surface with no bumps on it.

## flaw
Mum took the dress back to the shop because she found a **flaw** in it.

## flea
The dog scratched because a **flea** bit him.

## flee
The mice **flee** from the house when the cat comes in.

## flew
A bird **flew** past my window.

## float
1 Karen can **float** on her back in the pool.
2 At the carnival, the **float** carried the band through the streets.

3  Nazeem watched the **float** on her fishing line. ▼

**flood**

1  A **flood** is a lot of water that spreads over land that is usually dry.

2  The river **flooded** and the water was two feet deep in the village street.

**floor**

Pick up all the things off the **floor** and put them away.

**flour**

**Flour** is a powder used to make cakes, pastry and bread. ▼

**flower**

1  The petals of a **flower** are usually a pretty colour.

2  Daffodils should **flower** in the spring.

**flu**

I was in bed with **flu** on Thursday.

**fly**

1  There was one **fly** on the window and two **flies** on the light.

2  We watched the bird **fly** to its nest.

**for**

I've got a present **for** you.

**foreigner**

A **foreigner** is a person who comes from another country.

**fortunate**

Tracey was very **fortunate**. Her gran sent her £5 in a letter.

**fortunately**

**Fortunately** we arrived just in time to see the start of the play.

**foul**

1  "That was a **foul** – he kicked me!" the footballer shouted.

2  The day was so **foul** and wet we didn't go out at all.

**four**

Our cat had **four** kittens yesterday.

**fowl**
A **fowl** is any sort of bird that is kept for its meat and eggs. Hens and turkeys are **fowl.** ▾

**frays**
This cloth **frays** at the edges very easily.

**freeze**
Water **freezes** into ice when it is very cold.

**frieze**
We made a **frieze** of our holiday pictures around the room. ▾

**fur**
My cat licks its **fur** clean.

**furious**
Mr Cross was **furious** when we broke his window with our ball.

64

**gnaw** (say nor)
My dog likes to **gnaw** a bone. ▾

**gradual**
The slope was so **gradual** that we didn't realize at first that we were on a hill.

**gradually**
The water rose so **gradually** that we did not notice it.

**grate**
1   Phil will **grate** the cheese for the spaghetti.
2   A fire burned brightly in the **grate**.

**great**
We had a **great** surprise yesterday.

**groan**
We heard him **groan** and knew he must be badly hurt.

**ground**

1 The bottle fell to the **ground** and broke.

2 The cricket **ground** was empty in winter.

3 Wheat is **ground** into flour at a mill.

**grown**

1 Ramesh has **grown** three inches this year.

2 Only the **grown**-ups went to the party.

**guard**

1 We saw the **guards** outside the palace. ▾

2 Our dog **guards** the house when we're out.

3 It is important to have a **guard** around the fire when a small child is around.

**guess**

1 Can you **guess** where we are going next?

2 He didn't know the answer, so he **guessed** at it

**guide**

1 The **guide** showed us all the sights of the town.

2 The **guide**book tells us about this museum.

3 You can join the Girl **Guides** next year.

**hair**

Tariq washed his **hair** today.

**hare**

A **hare** is like a rabbit with long ears and big, strong back legs. ▾

**haunt**

The castle is supposed to be **haunted** by a headless ghost.

**heal**

The doctor said the cut would **heal** quickly.

**hear**

I can't **hear** you when you whisper.

**heard**

I **heard** strange sounds in the next room.

**heaviest**
A baby whale is the **heaviest** baby creature when it is born.

**heel**
1   Theresa's new shoes rubbed her **heel** until it was sore.
2   Mandy has very high **heels** on her shoes.

**heir** (say air)
Prince Charles is **heir** to the throne. One day he will be king.

**herd**
There is a small **herd** of brown cows in that field. ▼

**here**
Come **here** next to me.

**higher**
Put it on a **higher** shelf so that the baby can't reach it.

**hire**
Let's **hire** a boat and go out on the river.

**hoarse**
My voice was **hoarse** from shouting.

**hole**
Jack had a big **hole** in his sock.

**horn**
1   All the cars were blowing their **horns**.
2   I didn't like the look of that fierce bull with its sharp **horns**. ▼

**horse**
The wagon was pulled by two black **horses**.

**hour**
There are 60 minutes in one **hour** and 24 **hours** in one day.

**humorous**
He told us a very **humorous** story and we all laughed.

**humour**
Hari has a good sense of **humour**. He always sees the funny side of things.

**idle**
Sophie had an **idle** day doing nothing at all.

**idol**
Michael Jackson is the **idol** of all his fans. ▼

**I'll**
If you'll do this, **I'll** do that.

**imagination**
Use your **imagination** and think up a good story.

**imagine**
Sarah **imagined** that she was an explorer in the jungle. ▼

**immediately**
Come **immediately** or you'll be too late.

**important**
1  The head of our school is a very **important** person.
2  It is **important** that everyone is here on time or we'll miss the train.

**impossible**
It is **impossible** to tie your shoe-laces with your teeth.

**injury**
The goalkeeper couldn't play because of the **injury** to his foot.

**interest**

1 James has a great **interest** in birds.

2 Jeanne is very **interested** in cycle racing.

**interesting**

The book was so **interesting** that Chris went on reading it all night.

**invent**

The record player was **invented** in 1888. ▼

▶**invention**

The **invention** of the record player has changed people's lives in many ways.

**invitation**

Did you get the **invitation** asking you to Jane's party?

**invite**

Did you **invite** Caroline to your party?

**judo**

At **judo** classes I'm learning how to throw people.

**key**

1 He unlocked the door with a huge **key**.

2 The **key** on the map shows the signs for roads and rivers. ▼

3 She **keyed** in the program on her computer.

**kind**

1 My aunt was very **kind** to me while Mum was ill.

2 What **kind** of cake do you want?

**knead**

You **knead** the dough by working it with your hands.

**knew**

She **knew** the names of all the flowers in our garden.

**knight**

1 The king made him a **knight** for his bravery.

2 A **knight** is one of the pieces of a chess set.

## knock

1  I heard a loud **knock** at the front door.

2  Who is that **knocking** on my door?

3  He was **knocked** off his bike.

4  **Knock-knock**
Who's there?
Felix.
Felix who?
Felix my ice-cream,
I'll lick his too!

## knot

The sailor tied a **knot** in the rope. ▼

## know

I **know** that story because we read it at school.

## last

1  Manjit was the **last** person in the line.

2  I went to a film **last** week.

3  If you give them fresh water, these flowers will **last** a long time.

## law

Everyone must obey the **law**, or rules, of the country.

## layer

The cake had cream between each **layer**. ▼

## leak

That bucket will **leak** because it has a hole in it.

## leant

Roger **leant** against the wall and rested for a few minutes.

## leek

A **leek** is a long, green and white vegetable which tastes a bit like an onion. ▼

## left

1  Is it in my right hand or my **left**?

2  He **left** the book on the bus.

## lent

1  Lauren **lent** Matthew 50p to buy the toy.

2  **Lent** is the six weeks before Easter Sunday.

### lesson

My piano **lessons** are on Monday afternoons.

### lift

1 Can you **lift** it? It's heavy.
2 The **lift** took us straight to the top floor. ▾

### light

1 When Ann turned off the **light**, it was very dark.
2 This bag is very **light**. I can carry it easily.
3 Use the torch to **light** your way down the dark road.
4 Wear something **light** at night so that drivers can see you.

### line

1 Sally drew a wriggly **line** in the sand.
2 A long **line** of people waited outside the cinema.
3 The railway **line** ran through a forest.
4 The captain told her team to **line** up behind her.

### live (rhymes with give)

I used to **live** in Glasgow.

### live (rhymes with hive)

Jamila went to see her favourite pop group **live** at the town hall.

### loan

1 I only want your bike as a **loan**. I'll give it back soon.
2 Will you **loan** me your bike? I'll give it back tomorrow.

### lock

1 You will need the key to open the **lock** on my bicycle.
2 Please **lock** the door.
3 A **lock** of her hair was tied with a ribbon.
4 A **lock** is part of a canal or river between gates. ▾

### loose

I have got a **loose** tooth.

### lose

Put your money in your pocket or you will **lose** it.

## made
Gill **made** a lovely cake for her mother.

## maid
The princess asked her **maid** to clear the table.

## mail
Letters and parcels sent through the post are the **mail**.

## main
There's a lot of traffic on the **main** road near our house.

## male
No **male** animal lays eggs or gives birth to babies.

## manage
1   It was difficult but I **managed** to solve the problem.
2   My Dad **manages** our local football team.

## manager
My Mum is the **manager** of a record shop.

## mane
The horse had a shiny black **mane** and tail.

## manner
The doctor spoke to us in a very nice **manner**.

## manor
The old **manor** house stood in beautiful grounds. ▾

## mansion
The millionaire lived in a **mansion** in a large park.

## mare
A **mare** is a female horse and a foal is a baby horse.

## marriage
1   Gran and Grandad have had a happy **marriage** for 50 years.
2   I was a bridesmaid at my cousin's **marriage**.

## master
1   My Dad is a **master** at the high school. He teaches history there.
2   We all made copies from the **master** copy.
3   At last, he has **mastered** how to ride a bike.

## mayor
The **mayor** is in charge of the town council. ▼

## mean
1 I did **mean** to tell you but I totally forgot.
2 The word "mew" **means** to make the sound of a cat.
3 She was so **mean** she wouldn't share her sweets.

## meat
I like spaghetti with **meat** sauce.

## medal
The police officer was awarded a **medal** for bravery. ▼

## meddle
Don't **meddle** with the things on my desk, I've just tidied them.

## meet
My Mum and little sister **meet** me at the gate after school.

## meter
That **meter** measures how much electricity we use in our house.

## metre
Alex won the 100 **metre** race.

## milk
1 The **milk** we drink comes from cows.
2 The farmer **milks** the cows twice a day.

## mind
1 Have you made up your **mind** about what to give her?
2 Do you **mind** missing the film?
3 Hey, **mind** out! This kettle is very hot.

## mine
1 There's a **mine** near us where coal is mined from the ground. ▼

2 "That's **mine**!" said Dave, pointing to his bike.

**minute** (say min-it)
There are 60 seconds in one **minute** and 60 **minutes** in one hour.

**minute** (say my-newt)
The insect was so **minute** that she could hardly see it.

**mischief**
Lucy and Edward are always getting up to **mischief**, playing tricks on people.

**mischievous**
The **mischievous** monkey pulled the dog's tail.

**missed**
1   The ball narrowly **missed** the goal.
2   I **missed** him when he moved to Cardiff.

**mist**
There was **mist** in the valley and we had to drive slowly.

**mistake**
1   If you make any **mistakes** you must correct them.
2   I did it by **mistake**; I really didn't mean to.
3   How did you **mistake** my coat for yours? They are quite different.

**moan**
Don't **moan** and complain to me. It's not my fault.

**model**
1   Dad made a **model** of the ship and put it on the shelf.
2   My uncle has the latest **model** of that car.
3   My brother and sister were **models** in our school fashion show.
4   They **modelled** the clothes in the fashion show.
5   She was **modelling** an aeroplane out of clay.

**moor**
1   We love walking on the windy, deserted **moors**.▾

2   She **moored** the boat so that it wouldn't float away.

**more**
Can I have **more** cake, please?

**mown**
The lawn was **mown** last week.

73

## muscle

The **muscles** in your body control your movements. ▼

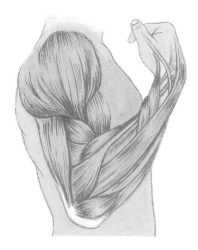

## mussel

A **mussel** is a creature with a black shell that lives in water.

## mysterious

A **mysterious** looking parcel lay on the table. We all wanted to know what was inside it.

## mystery

It remained a **mystery** to us. We never discovered how he had escaped.

## nail

1 Rose painted her finger**nails** bright red.

2 Kamla hit the **nail** with a hammer.

3 Brian **nailed** the pieces of wood together.

## name

1 My first **name** is Lucy and my last name is Robertson.

2 We **named** our puppy Tatty.

## necessary

It is **necessary** for us all to try very hard or we'll lose the match.

## need

I have grown so much that I **need** a new pair of shoes.

## new

Pat wore her **new** dress to the party yesterday.

## niece

Your brother's or sister's daughter is your **niece**.

## night

The moon and stars shine in the sky at **night**. ▼

**none**
Robert had lots of sweets but Nicola had **none.**

**nor**
Kate wants neither this cassette **nor** that one.

**not**
This is mine **not** yours.

**notice**
1  The **notice** about the painting competition was printed in the newspaper.▼

2  Paula **noticed** that the horse was lame.

**nuisance**
Richard is a **nuisance**. He talks when I want to read.

**nun**
The **nun** spoke to the class about her life in the convent.

**oar**
You need two **oars** to row a boat.▼

**object** (say *ob*-ject)
An **object** is anything that can be seen or touched.

**object** (say ob-*ject*)
They **object** to the new road being built so close to the school.

**occasion**
Birthdays are special **occasions**.

**occasionally**
We don't go there often but we do go **occasionally**.

**one**
My little sister can count from **one** to ten.

## operation

I went to hospital for an **operation** on my foot. ▼

## or

I'd like either beans **or** sausages.

## our

Would you like to come to **our** house for tea?

## pain

Sue was crying because of the **pain** in her tummy.

## paint

1 Suzanne mixed red with yellow **paint** to make orange.

2 Dave is **painting** a picture of the farm.

## pair

Leroy is very proud of his new **pair** of football boots.

## pane

Our ball broke a **pane** of glass in the greenhouse.

## pantomime

We went to the theatre to see the **pantomime** of "Pinocchio" this Christmas. ▼

## park

1 We go to the **park** to walk and play games.

2 Dad **parked** the car in the supermarket car park.

## parliament

The people who are chosen to make the laws of the country are the **parliament**.

## pass

1 We **pass** the library on the way to school.

2 Please **pass** me the jam. I can't reach it.

## passed

1 Derek **passed** the salt to Mike.

2 Laura **passed** her driving test.

3 We **passed** your house on our way here.

## past

1  It happened a long time ago in the **past**.

2  We walked **past** the church on our way to school.

## patience

He had to wait a long time and I admired his **patience**.

## patient

1  Although Gavin had to wait three hours, he was very **patient** and didn't get angry.

2  There were about 20 **patients** waiting in the doctor's surgery.

## pause

There was a short **pause** and then the noise started again.

## paw

We could see that the cat had hurt its **paw**. ▼

## paws

The cat licked all the milk off its **paws**.

## peace

1  People long for **peace** during a war.

2  Gemma wanted some **peace** and quiet so that she could read.

## peak

We reached the **peak** of the mountain after a long climb. ▼

## pear

The fruit salad was made of apples, **pears** and bananas.

## pedal

1  You push the **pedals** of a bicycle with your feet to make the wheels go round.

2  My little brother loves to **pedal** his tricycle along the path.

## peel

1 Put the **peel** of your orange in this bag.

2 I **peel** apples with a knife.

## peer

1 Lions **peer** through the bars at a zoo.

2 A **peer** is a member of the House of Lords.

## penalty

1 Our team was awarded a **penalty** because the other team broke the rules.

2 The **penalty** for being so naughty is that you won't go to the party.

## phrase

A group of words that belong together is a **phrase**: "the end of the road" is a **phrase**.

## piece

Would you like a **piece** of cake?

## pier

We walked to the end of the **pier** and looked out to sea. ▼

## place

1 Put the book back in the same **place**.

2 Save me a **place** in class.

3 **Place** your letters in this box.

## plaice

A **plaice** is a flat sea fish which is good to eat.

## plain

1 He wore a **plain** shirt and striped trousers.

2 Although she was a very **plain** kitten, Sammie grew into a beautiful cat.

3 Zebras were grazing on the African **plain**.

## plan

1 You can see your street on this **plan** of the town.

2 The Scouts **planned** what they would do during the summer holidays.

## plane

1 Can you see that **plane** in the sky?

2 A **plane** tree has large leaves.

3 He used a **plane** to make the wood smooth. ▼

## plant

1 Trees, vegetables and flowers are all **plants**.

2 Harjinder **planted** some cress seeds in a pot.

## play

1 Our class is acting a short **play** for open day.

2 Ramzan and Philip enjoy **playing** tennis.

3 Rosa **plays** the trumpet in our band.

## poison

1 There is enough **poison** here to kill an elephant.

2 Mum **poisoned** the slugs with a spray.

## poisonous

Those wild mushrooms are **poisonous** so you shouldn't eat them.

## polish

1 Use this **polish** to make the table shine.

2 At Christmas, Dad **polished** the silver mug until it shone brightly.

## poor

1 When you are **poor** you do not have much money.

2 The teacher told her that her work was **poor** and that she must try harder.

## potion

The wizard gave the princess a magic **potion** that made her able to fly. ▾

## pour

1 **Pour** the milk into the cups.

2 It **poured** with rain all day.

## practice

I go to football **practice** every Monday.

## practise

I **practise** football on Mondays.

## pray

We **pray** in assembly each morning. ▾

## prefer

I **prefer** marmalade to jam but my brother said he **preferred** jam.

**prepare**
They **prepared** the hall for the concert by putting out the chairs.

**present** (say *prez*-ent)
1  There were lots of **presents** under the Christmas tree. ▼

2  Our teacher is away at **present**; she'll be back next week.

**present** (say pre-*zent*)
The mayor will **present** the prizes after the sports.

**pretend**
Let's **pretend** that we're asleep. Then he'll go away.

**prey**
1  A bird of **prey** hunts small animals.
2  The lionness hunted her **prey** through the long grass. ▼

**principal**
Rani was the **principal** dancer in the ballet because he was so good.

**principle**
The **principles** of football are its basic rules.

**professor**
A **professor** is a senior teacher in a college.

**program**
She keyed in a new **program** on her computer.

**prove**
Can you **prove** that this is your watch and not hers?

**provide**
Can you **provide** enough food for the whole class?

**quarrel**
We **quarrelled** over who should have the last biscuit.

**quay**
Ships are loaded at the **quay**.

**queue**

1  A **queue** is a line of people, one behind the other.

2  We were all **queuing** up to catch the bus. ▾

 **Rr**

**race**

1  I'll **race** you to the end of the road.

2  Max came second in the egg-and-spoon **race**.

**rain**

1  The **rain** stopped and the sun came out.

2  It **rained** all day today.

**raw**

The meat is **raw**. We need to cook it.

**read** (rhymes with need)

I'm going to **read** a comic.

**read** (rhymes with bed)

Helen **read** the poem aloud to us yesterday.

**real**

This is a **real** diamond not a pretend one.

**realize**

Do you **realize** that we've been here two hours already?

**rear**

1  We like sitting in the **rear** of the bus not in the front.

2  The horse **reared** up on its back legs. ▾

**receive**

Did you **receive** my letter in the post today?

**recognize**

I don't **recognize** anyone; I haven't met any of them before.

**red**

The garden was full of **red** flowers: roses, poppies and tulips.

**reed**

This **reed** grows near the stream.

## reel

1 I need a **reel** of film for my camera.

2 Wind in your fishing **reel**; I think you've caught something!▼

## reign (say rain)

1 We hope the Queen will **reign** for a long time.

2 The Albert Hall was built in Queen Victoria's **reign**.

## rein (say rain)

1 She led the young horse on a long **rein**.▼

2 You **rein** in your horse to slow it down.

## reliable

Hamish is very **reliable**. You can always trust him to do what he promises.

## repeat

The teacher asked us to **repeat** the words after her.

## rhyme (rhymes with time)

1 The word horse **rhymes** with force and coarse.

2 This is a **rhyme**:
"Ring-a-ring o' roses
    A pocketful of posies."

## rhythm

Pop music usually has a strong **rhythm** or beat.

## right

1 Most people hold a pen in their **right** hand.

2 It is not **right** to be rude.

3 Tick the **right** answer.

4 She turned **right** around to face the other way.

## ring

1 Draw a **ring** around your name.

2 My Dad wears a **ring** on his finger.

3 Did you hear the phone **ring** just then?

4 Please **ring** the door bell.

5 Did you **ring** up the doctor for me?

**road**

We walked along the **road** to the shops.

**roar**

We can hear the lions and tigers in the zoo **roar** at night.

**rode**

She **rode** her bicycle along the track to the farm.

**rose**

1    We picked a pretty pink **rose** in the garden. ▼

2    A strange creature **rose** up from the waves.

**row** (rhymes with show)

The hall was filled with **rows** of chairs.

**row** (rhymes with how)

There are **rows** all the time when the boys are both at home.

## Ss

**safe**

1    It is **safe** to swim here because the water isn't deep.

2    The bank manager locked the gold coins in the **safe**. ▼

**safely**

All the crew got **safely** ashore after the shipwreck.

**safety**

A helicopter lifted them to **safety**.

**sail**

1    The wind caught the **sail** and the yacht raced faster. ▼

2    Let's go for a **sail** on the lake.

3    The boat **sailed** across the sea.

**sale**

Dad bought a new jacket at the **sale** for only £5.

**sauce**

I like ice-cream with hot chocolate **sauce**.

83

**saw**

1  I **saw** a magpie in my garden this morning.

2  She cut the tree into logs with a **saw**.

**sawed**

She **sawed** the log in two. ▼

**scene**

1  The police were quickly at the **scene** of the accident.

2  Joanna only appeared in the last **scene** of the play.

3  He makes a terrible **scene** when he has to go to bed.

**scent**

1  Mum put on some lovely **scent** to go to the party.

2  The **scent** of the roses filled the air.

3  The hounds could follow the **scent** of the fox.

**scream**

1  We heard a **scream** and ran to see who had been hurt.

2  Alice **screamed** when she burnt her fingers.

**sea**

Fish swim in the **sea** and ships sail on the **sea**.

**seal**

1  A **seal** is a furry animal that lives in the sea and also on the land. ▼

2  **Seal** that envelope with some glue or the letter will fall out.

**sealing**

I am **sealing** the envelope with some glue.

**seam**

I tore the **seam** of my shirt on the swing. ▼

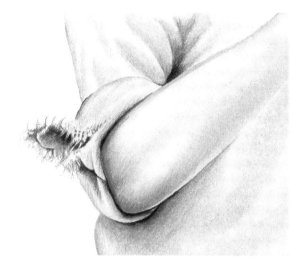

**seas**

Fishermen don't like to go out in rough **seas**.

**second**

1  There are 60 **seconds** in one minute.
2  Josh won **second** prize in the race.

**see**

I can **see** the church from my window.

**seem**

I know it was only a film but it did **seem** real.

**seen**

A fox was **seen** in our street last night.

**sees**

Our cat is startled when it **sees** itself in the mirror.

**seize**

They **seized** the thief by the collar!

**sell**

They **sell** marbles in that shop.

**seller**

The balloon-**seller** had silver and gold balloons.

**sense**

1  Dogs have a good **sense** of hearing.
2  Grandpa has a very good **sense** of humour.
3  If he had any **sense** he wouldn't have done that.

**sent**

I **sent** Gran a letter last week.

**separate** (say separ-*ate*)
Can you **separate** the knives from the forks?

**separate** (say *sep*-arate)
The model came in **separate** parts and Kavita had to fix them together. ▼

**serial**

I missed the last part of the **serial** on television.

**serious**

1 Joe is a **serious** boy. He is thoughtful and careful.

2 Be **serious** – this is not something to laugh at.

3 There has been a **serious** accident on the motorway.

**seriously**

1 She spoke to him **seriously** about his rudeness.

2 My aunt was **seriously** hurt in a car crash.

**severe**

1 The old man looked very **severe** and told us not to play near the road.

2 Douglas is away from school with a **severe** cold.

**sew**

I'm **sewing** on this button.

**share**

Can I **share** your book?

**shear**

The wool that they **shear** off sheep is made into sweaters.▼

**sheer**

It was a **sheer** drop of 50 metres.

**sheriff**

The **sheriff** arrested the cowboys for stealing cattle.

**shoot**

1 **Shoot** at the goal now!

2 At the fair, we tried **shooting** at coconuts.

3 This plant has grown a few new **shoots**.▼

**shop**

1 We went to that **shop** to buy shoes.

2 Mum and Dad like to **shop** in the new supermarket.

**shore**

The waves broke on the sea-**shore**.

**shot**

1 At the fair, Sharon **shot** at the target.

2 We heard the gun **shot** from half a mile away.

## show

1 Can you **show** me how to mend my bike?

2 We brought our dogs, cats and other pets to school for the pet **show**.

3 Grandpa took us to a **show** in the village hall. There was singing and dancing.

## sight

1 His **sight** is good. He can see much further than me.

2 The **sight** of blood makes me feel funny.

## sink

1 Dad washes up in the kitchen **sink**.

2 A stone **sinks** if you drop it into water.

## site

They were building a new house on the building **site**. ▼

## sleep

1 The baby **sleeps** in a cot in my bedroom.

2 I had 11 hours' **sleep** last night.

## sleigh

Reindeer pull Santa's **sleigh**. ▼

## slide

1 We love to **slide** on the ice in winter.

2 We took it in turns going down the **slide**.

3 Alison is wearing a **slide** in her hair.

4 Mr Okwesa showed us **slides** about Nigeria.

## smell

1 I can **smell** dinner being cooked in the kitchen.

2 There was a nasty **smell** in the garage.

## so

1 Ian had been naughty **so** he couldn't come with us.

2 She was **so** upset she cried.

**soar**

We watched the plane **soar** into the sky.

**soared**

The eagle **soared** high above the hills.

**some**

I want **some** of those cherries, not all of them.

**son**

Mary helped her **son** with his homework.

**sore**

My knee is **sore** where I cut it.

**sort**

1   Can you **sort** these socks into their different pairs?▾

2   What **sort** of ice-cream do you like best?

**source**

We found the **source** of the stream in a valley.

**sow** (rhymes with toe)

Errol **sowed** all the seeds in his garden.

**sow** (rhymes with cow)

A **sow** is a female pig.▾

**spare**

1   There's a **spare** tyre in the boot of our car.

2   Can you **spare** a few hours to help us?

**spear**

1   A **spear** is a long pole with a sharp point on the end.▾

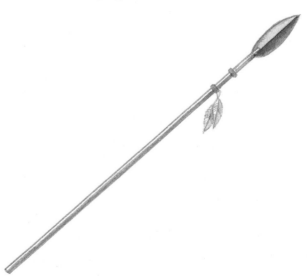

2   **Spear** a leaf with that stick.

**spoke**

1 She **spoke** to us about her work in the hospital.

2 A **spoke** is a wire or rod that goes from the centre to the rim of a wheel.

**spring**

1 When **spring** comes, the plants begin to grow again.

2 The **springs** in the bicycle seat make it comfortable to ride on.

3 This river starts from a **spring** in that valley.

4 Our dog likes to hide and **spring** out on us.

**stair**

Don't leave your shoes on the **stairs** or someone might trip.

**stake**

He put a **stake** in the ground and fixed on the for sale sign.

**stalk** (rhymes with fork)

1 Only one leaf was left on the **stalk**.

2 My cat **stalks** birds.

3 He **stalked** out of the room in a temper.

**stare**

1 Everyone **stared** at him.

2 I could almost feel Chad's **stare** from across the room.

**start**

1 The runners waited at the **start**. ▾

2 Please **start** at the beginning.

**steak** (rhymes with brake)

Dad's favourite dinner is **steak** and chips.

**steal**

The birds **steal** fruit off our trees.

**steel**

**Steel** is a strong, shiny metal which is made from iron.

**step**

1 Don't **step** on my record or you'll break it.

2 We go down three **steps** into the garden.

**stile**

We climbed over the **stile**. ▾

**storey**

I live on the fourth **storey** of the block of flats.

**story**

Please tell me the **story** of the three bears again.

**stuff**

1   What sort of **stuff** did you use to make the toy?

2   **Stuff** the pillow with rags.

3   Rob was **stuffing** his shoes into the suitcase. ▼

**style**

Our teacher had his hair cut in a new **style** this term.

**succeed**

I think I will only **succeed** if I work hard.

**success**

The play was a great **success**. The audience cheered.

**suite**

We have a three piece **suite** in our lounge. ▼

**sum**

Can you do this **sum**? 6 + 6 = ☐

**sun**

The **sun** was shining brightly.

**sure**

Are you **sure** you're right?

**sweet**

1   My favourite **sweets** are toffees.

2   If you drink **sweet** things they could harm your teeth.

3   After our omelette we had apple pie as a **sweet**.

**swing**

1   Push the **swing** gently or she might fall off it.

2   Shut the window or it will **swing** open in the wind.

3   Let's **swing** the boat round so that we don't hit that rock.

**switch**

1 Turn the light **switch** on.

2 **Switch** on the hall light.

3 Emily and Polly **switched** places and sat in each other's chairs.

**sword**

The knight pointed his **sword**.▼

**tail**

A squirrel has a big fluffy **tail**.▼

**tale**

She told us a **tale** of long ago and far away.

**talk**

1 Let's **talk** about our holidays.

2 We had a **talk** about snakes at school today.

**their**

Those are **their** books not ours.

**there**

Look over **there** and you'll see some sheep.

**they're**

Today **they're** playing basketball.

**threw**

Judy **threw** the ball to Paul.

**throne**

The king sat on his **throne**.▼

**through**

We saw the train go **through** the tunnel.

**thrown**

Have you **thrown** away the label from this packet?

**tide**
The **tide** is the rising and falling of the sea, which happens twice each day.

**tied**
She **tied** a bow in her hair. ▼

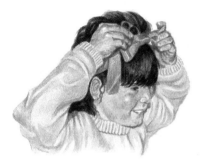

**tire**
Running around so much will **tire** you. Sit down and rest.

**to**
1  We're going **to** school now.
2  I am wet **to** the skin.

**toe**
You have ten **toes**. ▼

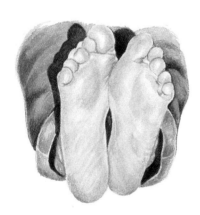

**too**
1  Don't take **too** much.
2  May we go **too**?

**tow**
The break-down van will **tow** the car to the garage.

**train**
1  The **train** left the station on time. ▼

2  We **trained** our dog well.
3  The bride's **train** was held by the two boys.

**two**
You have **two** eyes and **two** ears.

**tyre**
The **tyres** on the wheels of my bike are made of rubber. ▼

92

## Uu

**ugliest**
When we made masks we each tried to make ours the **ugliest**.

**understand**
Listen carefully and then you'll **understand** what to do.

**use** (rhymes with goose)
1 The scissors aren't any **use**. They're blunt.
2 After the accident, he lost the **use** of his right arm.

**use** (rhymes with lose)
1 Can I **use** your scissors to cut this paper?
2 I've **used** up all the paint. The tube is empty.
3 We **used** to live in London.

## Vv

**vain**
1 He is very **vain** and is always looking at himself in the mirror.
2 She tried in **vain** to mend the bike but the bolts were too rusty.

**vanish**
The fairy **vanished** and we never saw her again.

**vein**
A **vein** is a narrow tube in your body. **Veins** carry blood to your heart. ▾

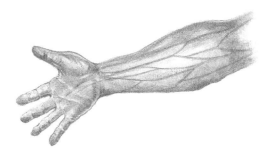

## Ww

**wade**
Let's **wade** through the stream.

**wail**
Our dog will **wail** if we leave him behind.

**waist**
He wore a red belt around his **waist**.

**wait**
We can **wait** here for the bus. It will be here in 10 minutes.

**walk**
1 We **walk** to school in the morning.
2 Let's go for a **walk** in the park.

**war**
The army is trained to fight in a **war**.

## warn

I **warn** you not to play there. It is very dangerous.

## waste

1 Don't **waste** your time doing that. It won't work.

2 I threw it in the **waste**-paper basket.

## watch

1 Can I **watch** television?

2 You've got a **watch**. Can you tell me the time, please?

## water

1 After so much rain, there was **water** all over the school playground.

2 We won't need to **water** the garden today, after the rain.

## wave

1 We watched the **waves** breaking on the sea-shore. ▼

2 We **waved** our hands to say goodbye.

3 Dad gave us a final **wave** as we left home.

## way

1 Do you know the **way** to go home?

2 Watch me and you'll see the **way** it is done.

## weak

The sick woman was too **weak** to sit up.

## wear

1 I'm **wearing** my old shoes.

2 I didn't want to **wear** out the batteries so I turned my torch off.

## weather

What will the **weather** be like today? Do you think it will rain?

## weave

Our teacher showed us how to **weave** cloth on the loom. ▼

## we'd

**We'd** only just arrived at the cinema when the film began.

## weed

That's a **weed**. We don't want it in the flower-bed.

**week**
There are seven days in a **week** and four **weeks** in a month.

**weigh**
1   Let's **weigh** it to see how heavy it is.
2   How much does it **weigh**?

**weighed**
We **weighed** the baby and she **weighed** 3.5 kilos. ▼

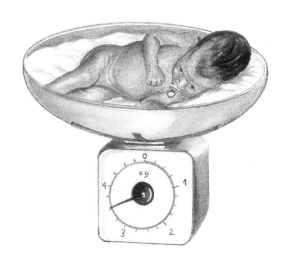

**weight**
1   The baby's **weight** is 3.5 kilos.
2   We put another **weight** on the scales.

**we'll**
If you like, **we'll** come too.

**were**
We **were** very pleased with our party yesterday.

**we've**
Today **we've** been to the park.

**whale**
A **whale** is a very large mammal that lives in the sea. ▼

**wheel**
1   Cars, bicycles and some machines have **wheels**. ▼

2   You can **wheel** your bicycle along the path.

**where**
Let's decide **where** to go today.

**whether**
Tim asked **whether** or not we wanted to go with him.

**which**
Choose **which** of these two books you want.

**whine**
Our dog **whines** when it's sad.

**whined**
Our puppy **whined** loudly.

**whistle**
1   Can you **whistle** this tune?
2   The referee blew his **whistle** for half-time. ▾

**whole**
1   We ate the **whole** cake; we didn't leave any crumbs.
2   Swallow the tablet **whole**.

**wind** (rhymes with tinned)
In autumn, the **wind** blows and the leaves fall down. ▾

**wind** (rhymes with blind)
1   **Wind** the clock with this key to make it go. ▾

2   Nicole will **wind** the wool into a ball.

**wine**
She gave my parents **wine** to drink.

**witch**
The **witch** in the story did some wicked things.

**won**
Our horse **won** the race.

**wood**
1   She carved the toy from a piece of **wood**.
2   Don't go into the dark **wood**.

**wore**
We all **wore** our best clothes for the party.

**work**
1   Have you finished the **work** I gave you?
2   Mum and Dad both go to **work** in the morning.
3   If we **work** hard we'll finish this soon.

**worn**

1 I should have **worn** my old clothes today.

2 The carpet was very **worn** and dirty.

3 We were **worn** out after our busy day.

**would**

I said I **would** be late.

**wound** (rhymes with sound)

Amarjit **wound** the rope around the tree.

**wound** (say wooned)

The knife had made a nasty **wound** on his hand.

**wrap**

I **wrapped** her present in paper.

**wreck**

1 The **wreck** of the ship was washed up on the shore. ▼

2 The plants were **wrecked** by the storm. Mum and Dad will have to start their garden again.

**wring**

We'll **wring** all the water out of the wet clothes.

**write**

Please **write** your name in this birthday card.

**X-ray**

The doctor took an **X-ray** of my arm to see if it was broken.

**yoke**

A **yoke** is put over the necks of oxen to help them pull a cart.

**yolk** (rhymes with joke)

The round yellow part of an egg is called the **yolk**.

**you're**

If you don't hurry **you're** going to be late.

**your**

Is that **your** coat with the hood?

**zebra**

We saw **zebras** at the zoo.